knowing
WHO I AM

ALSO BY NIANELL

knowing
WHO I AM

love yourself and make a difference

NIANELL

HAY HOUSE, INC.
Carlsbad, California • New York City
London • Sydney • Johannesburg
Vancouver • Hong Kong • New Delhi

Published and distributed in the United States by: Hay House, Inc.: www.hayhouse.com®
Published and distributed in Australia by: Hay House Australia Pty. Ltd.: www.hayhouse
.com.au • **Published and distributed in the United Kingdom by:** Hay House UK, Ltd.: www
.hayhouse.co.uk • **Distributed in Canada by:** Raincoast: www.raincoast.com • **Published in
India by:** Hay House Publishers India: www.hayhouse.co.in

Project management by Elzanne Loest

Edited by Marisa Robson

Originally published by Struik Inspirational (ISBN: 978-1-4153-1278-0)
A division of New Holland Publishing (South Africa) (Pty) Ltd
Cornelis Struik House
80 McKenzie Street
Cape Town 8001
South Africa

Library of Congress Control Number: 2012941679

Tradepaper ISBN: 978-1-4019-4022-5
Digital ISBN: 978-1-4019-4023-2

15 14 13 12   4 3 2 1
1st Hay House edition, October 2012

Printed in the United States of America

SUSTAINABLE
FORESTRY
INITIATIVE
Certified Chain of Custody
Promoting Sustainable Forestry
www.sfiprogram.org
SFI-01268

SFI label applies to the text stock

With love to my three precious little angels,
Kaeley, Jade, and Tayden

CONTENTS

INTRODUCTION

KEEPING IT REAL

This is a special hello to you—my readers and supporters. Thank you so much for reading my book! I do hope that I will get to meet all of you someday. You are all very special to me, and I would really love to give you a big hug and thank you in person! I love hugging people. The endorphins that your body produces when you hug someone make you feel happy, and I really love feeling happy—who doesn't?

I've always known that I would write a book one day, but I never expected it to happen so early in my life. I thought people might take my writing more seriously when I was older—perhaps in my 50s or 60s—but the door opened sooner than expected and I decided to enter.

I started to write this book around the end of August 2010. During the months that followed, I had mixed feelings, and on two occasions even had second thoughts about writing it. My deadline was April 15, 2011, and at times I found myself wondering whether I would ever be able to meet it … but if you are reading this, it means that I made it—which is awesome!

I had never written a book before, but as a successful singer/songwriter, I've written a lot of other things (like lyrics), and I realized that my minimum requirement of 60,000 words was going to take some time. I had only written 15,000 by November 17, 2010! At the time I was also busy reading a 150,000-word book that had taken the author about nine years to write. Right there, I needed to remind myself not to compare. Comparing is just me setting myself up to feel inadequate … which past experience has taught me can lead to nothing positive.

It might have been less stressful if writing this book had been the only thing on my plate, but being a mother to three 3-year-olds, being a professional musician doing about 110 shows a year, and working on two new albums at the same time made my schedule very tight indeed. Aside from struggling to find the time to write, I also found the process very demanding. Writing a book about being alive, loving yourself, accepting your self-worth, and accepting who you are makes you *discover* more about who you are. It also means revisiting who you were, letting go, forgiving, learning, growing, and researching. I found all of this very intense and time-consuming.

However, the real reason why I sometimes felt like quitting was my doubt that anything I wrote would ever really capture what I have awakened to or the huge number of discoveries I made about myself during this short time.

Yet I am here for a reason. I believe that writing this book is part of that reason … and that is why I convinced myself to continue when I felt like quitting. I know that what I have written will have flaws, but it comes from my heart. It has been written with honesty, love, and compassion, not to convince, impress, or change anyone.

Initially, I didn't want to feature myself in this book at all. It was important to me that people would be touched by what I've learned about life so far rather than focusing on me. I had a great title and cover in mind, and *my* face and *my* name were not part of it … that all changed when I gave some serious thought to the discussion I had with my publisher after our first meeting.

I love reading … and believe me, I have read many books in my life. One of the things I enjoy most is getting to know the authors and reading about their own experiences—or just reading about real-life experiences in general. I can relate to that … it keeps it real for me. I realized that was exactly what I needed to do with this book: Keep it real and write about what I know best—my life, my experiences, and the lessons I have learned so far. So without further ado, allow me to introduce myself!

ABOUT MYSELF

My birth name is So**nia** Aletta **Nel**, but I am better known as Nianell, which is my stage name. I was born on September 25, 1971, in the town of Omaruru, Namibia, Africa. Omaruru is a tiny village. In fact, it is so small that I was the only baby in the hospital! My parents and grandparents farmed together in the area, but that didn't last very long, as my grandfather and father are both very strong-

willed (I have to confess, I take after them in that respect). Shortly after I was born, we moved to Windhoek, the capital city of Namibia, where I grew up. My father rejoined the police force, and my mother continued her career as a primary-school teacher. Both my parents were passionate about their jobs and excelled in their chosen fields. I am very proud of them.

Music was always part of our lives. We didn't have television transmission in Namibia until I was about ten years old, so we entertained ourselves as a family by making music together—my father playing guitar while the rest of us sang along. By the time I was eight years old, my singing voice was so well developed that I sounded like a grown woman. Interestingly, we had a tenant who used to pay me two rand (the equivalent of about one U.S. dollar) just to sing for him. I was born to write music and sing. I believe music chose me.

Marhess van Rooyen

I went to two different primary schools: Van Rhyn and Pionierspark Primary School. I graduated from Academia High School in 1989, and in 1990 managed to secure a scholarship to study light music at the former Pretoria Technikon (now Tshwane University of Technology) in South Africa. I was following my dream of making my living from music.

I earned my diploma in Light Music in 1994 and found a part-time job teaching music at Wierdapark Primary School. Although I loved children and teaching, my heart longed for the stage, and I was no longer satisfied with the small gigs I did here and there. Performing has always been my passion. So I decided to take the big step: quit my part-time job and do what I was most passionate about. It meant saying goodbye to my small but steady income, but at least I would be doing what I loved.

I met my wonderful husband, Andrew Thompson, in 1997, and we were married on South Africa's Freedom Day, April 27, 2000. Marrying Andrew confirmed my belief that there is freedom in getting married to the right person.

Marihess van Rooyen

Seven years later we were blessed with the birth of our lovely triplet girls, Kaeley, Jade, and Tayden. They were born on July 30, 2007, and will always be the biggest miracle in our lives. We fell pregnant naturally after trying for just one month, and it was exactly what we had prayed for. (I still don't understand why here in South Africa they talk about "falling pregnant." Nothing falls—everything just rises!) I had always wanted three children, but had never been able to imagine myself going through three pregnancies, so I am extremely thankful for the way things turned out. I even wrote a song called "I Know I'm Lucky" just before I discovered I was pregnant. I believe that singing those positive words over and over can only attract more amazing experiences into my life.

KNOWING WHO I AM

Looking at all this biographical information, it's easy to come to a conclusion about who I am: a 40-year-old woman with a husband, three children, and a successful career in the southern African music industry. I also always thought this was who I was. For many years I believed I was nothing without my ability to sing and write songs. I had defined myself by my voice and music. This put my sense of self-worth at the mercy of public opinion; I was nothing if the public didn't approve of or support my talent.

Measuring my own value in this way, I had a serious uphill battle for many years, during which I constantly searched for and doubted myself and my abilities. I didn't even know how to conduct myself in a crowd if I wasn't there in my capacity as a performing artist. I didn't believe that people would like me or accept me unless I could do something to impress them, and deep down, I was terrified. When I look at my little girls now, I often see myself in them, trying so hard to be noticed and loved. They pull out every trick in the book to gain acceptance.

Jacques Stander

To be honest, it never crossed my mind that I could just *be.* I always thought I had to *do* something, *achieve* something, or *prove* something to be accepted by others. I was relying on other people's acceptance in order to be able to love and accept myself.

From the time I was very little, I felt that I had an important purpose here on Earth and spent the greater part of 40 years trying to figure out what it was … chasing after what I thought it was.

The wonderful thing is that along this journey I came to understand who I am and why I am here. Thankfully, I came to realize

Marihess van Rooyen

that who I am is not determined by what I do or achieve, or by the approval I get from others—but this is very easy to forget when life's pressure is on. That is why I am deeply grateful to have this book, as well as the songs that come to me; they are a constant reminder of who I really am.

I invite you to join me on my life journey. In the process, hopefully you will discover who *you* really are and why it is so important to love yourself just as you are.

CHAPTER ONE

LOVING MYSELF AND ACCEPTING MY WORTH

L oving myself has always been one of my biggest challenges. When I started researching self-love about ten years ago, I discovered that there are many different ways to love or not love yourself.

For instance, you might have self-confidence, but you can have low self-worth at the same time. This might sound like a contradiction, but let me try to explain by telling you about my high school years.

CONFIDENCE

Through the years I have taught myself to forget the bad stuff and hold on to the good stuff—but it's really the bad stuff that helps us grow into better and stronger human beings in the end.

I experienced a lot of resistance in high school. One positive thing this taught me was perseverance. I appeared outwardly confident when I got up on that school stage and sang my heart out while the schoolboys in the front row rolled on the floor with laughter, and also when I put my hand up in class and pretended not to hear some boy whispering the taunt, "Sing us a song, sing us a song."

Very few people in my school made a fuss about my singing—most of the time I felt that my talent counted against me. Some of my music teachers told me that I didn't really have what it took to have a future in music. One teacher sent me to see the deputy headmaster, who told me to stop taking piano lessons because there were children who were willing to work harder at it than I was. I really did try my best, but found the theory of music very hard to understand. I remember sitting at home in the afternoons, going on imaginary trips in my head, trying to escape from my theory homework.

Thankfully there were also teachers who did recognize my talent, and I will remain forever grateful to them for their support during that time. I was part of a two-piece band with one of them, and we performed at a number of local events. One morning I passed a classroom and heard the teacher telling her class that our "band" might be performing at their prom. I stopped to listen when I heard my name, only to hear the whole class moan in protest. The teacher agreed with them and reassured them that she would sort it out.

We didn't play at the prom. I was relieved—it would have been very hard for me to muster that kind of confidence.

I didn't get the leading roles or win the competitions. I also wasn't popular at all; in fact, I was relatively odd. I recently saw a photo of a school outing. There I was, dressed up in my Sunday best while everybody else wore shorts and sneakers. Thankfully I was totally oblivious to the fact that I was the odd one out; I thought everyone else was a little strange. Ignorance is bliss, and I remained in that bubble for a very long time.

I couldn't wait to finish school so that I could do what I loved, and I am truly blessed that my parents understood me and gave me the space to grow.

They allowed me to do performances with our "band" in my spare time, and in 11th grade I managed to get a solo gig performing at a little restaurant not far from home. Every Friday night I drove there on my scooter with my 12-string guitar tightly tucked between my legs. In the beginning my fingers bled from all the playing—I wasn't used to playing a steel-string guitar so often—but after a while my fingertips got used to it. I would have preferred to accompany myself on the piano, but couldn't fit my piano onto my scooter.

I was measuring my value by people's reactions, responses, and support.

My folks would wait up for me whenever I played, and when I got home, we would sit in the kitchen and eat the take-out steak and chips I received as part of my payment. I earned 50 rand per night plus a meal in those days.

I also learned how to prepare a delicious snail dish by helping out in the kitchen during my breaks. I did this for free because I felt safer in the kitchen than I did with the restaurant's customers. It's ironic that I was confident enough to sing for people, but not enough to mingle with them.

I spent a lot of time hiding away at school. If I found an open classroom during break time, I would just sit there, playing the piano and trying to sing myself away. Sometimes I would even skip a gym class (or any other class that I didn't think was important) if I saw the music classroom open and empty.

I was also the in-between entertainment for our school's revue group; I entertained the audience while they did costume changes. Once, while I was hiding behind the piano during a rehearsal break, I heard one teacher trying to convince another to cut some of the songs I sang because she felt they didn't work. Those were my best songs, and I was relieved when the second teacher took my side.

Unfortunately, when you hide away, you hear a lot of things you're not meant to.

Although my experiences at school taught me to appear confident and to persevere, they also surreptitiously gnawed away at my self-worth. I was measuring my value by people's reactions, responses, and support.

I don't harbor any anger or resentment toward anyone involved in my high school experience, because I have taken responsibility for my part in it. I have realized that I never made it easy for anyone to understand or get to know me since I preferred my own company. I can't blame them for not accepting me, either, because I didn't accept them. Gifted children are often very challenging to teach and often get overlooked by teachers in their early stages.

Always try to put yourself in someone else's shoes; that way their actions become easier to understand.

Always try to put yourself in someone else's shoes; that way their actions become easier to understand. I know you also have a story of unfair or unkind treatment; we all do. We need to treasure those valuable experiences, learn and grow from them, be thankful for them, take responsibility for our part in them, and then let them go.

FORGIVENESS

When I was in ninth grade and about 15 years old, I went to veld school, which is like a field trip where you spend time in nature and do team building and activities to build character. It was an event I will never forget. I was very excited. I love the outdoors, and this was going to be a great adventure! I had gone to veld school for the first time in fifth grade and that had been amazing, so I was expecting to have a great time again.

Everything started out okay. On the first day we did obstacle courses and exercises individually and in teams. I really enjoyed those and also excelled in them. The teachers and camp leader observed us closely. Afterward, I realized they had been picking teams.

The next day we were taught how to use a compass (I still don't know how to work one—thank goodness for my GPS!). When the camp leader asked us if we all understood, there were only two of us who didn't, and it took a lot of courage for me to raise my hand; the camp leader didn't seem like a very approachable guy. He explained the whole thing to us again, in exactly the same way as he had done before.

Now here's a great tip for teachers: If someone doesn't understand something after you've explained it, there's every chance that person will still struggle if you explain it the same way a second time. I think that what makes a teacher great is the ability to find new and inventive ways of describing things ... that, and the ability to recognize and encourage people's strengths.

Every person is unique and needs things explained in a particular way. I often don't understand conventional explanations, and found school very difficult. In those days, it was designed for a specific way of thinking, and that's probably why it was suggested that I do a secretarial course after graduating from high school—my creativity and entrepreneurial skills weren't recognized. I think I would have lasted one month as a secretary; after that, I would either be fired or running the company!

Anyway, back to the compass. I didn't understand it the second time, either, but the camp leader told me, "*Jou saak is jou saak.*" Basically, this meant that it was now my problem, not his. I think it did become his problem the next day when I went missing overnight. I walked for an entire day in search of my destination and had to spend the whole night alone in the harsh Namibian wild without any food or water.

They had dropped everyone off in pairs before sunrise that morning, except me and the other girl who didn't understand. She and I were dropped separately, after the others, and were given coordinates for a destination that we had to find using our compasses.

Needless to say, I headed off in the wrong direction. I remember thinking, while climbing a high cliff, that the camp leader must have had a very high impression of me to have given me such a dangerous route.

I had spent a lot of time in the bush with my family, camping with my father, and because of that I could handle myself well in the situation. Only when it became dark and I still hadn't met up with my team did I realize I was lost.

Feeling very afraid all alone in the dark, I zipped myself into my sleeping bag and wondered if anyone was looking for me as I listened to the night noises. I didn't sleep. As soon as it was light, I set off to find my way back to the main camp, abandoning the compass in favor of my sense of direction.

By lunchtime I'd found it. I couldn't understand why I wasn't welcomed back with open arms, but it soon became clear that I was accused of deliberately getting lost to attract attention. I'm not sure why anyone would have thought I would choose to spend a night alone in the dangerous Namibian jungle.

That night we were all placed in groups armed with a team name, a team song, a team flag, and a team story that we had worked on all afternoon. I had been the creative mind behind a lot of my team's work. After our presentations, the camp leader asked each team to make the *droogmaker* (slacker) in the group stand up. My group was

We can only love others and ourselves unconditionally when we forgive.

perfect—no, really, I mean *perfect*. They were good-looking and bright, and eventually all became prefects (except me, of course). Needless to say, they all pointed me out. Something broke inside me as I stood there, labeled "slacker" and listening to the camp leader telling everyone that we slackers were the ones who never did our part, the ones who just rode on the other team members' backs.

One of the girls in our team (who eventually became our head girl) went to the camp leader afterward and admitted that I had done more than my share for the team; they had only picked me because I was the brunt of an occasional joke—and because I had gotten lost.

On the last day of veld school, we all had to line up in front of the camp leader's office to go in and see him one by one. That day he told me I needed to get professional help because he couldn't figure me out at all. If this weren't bad enough, some of the teachers who had accompanied us told my story to the older children at school. Soon everybody believed I had gotten lost on purpose. High school wasn't kind to me before, but after veld school it became worse. I relived this bad experience over and over in my head, nurturing my pain and humiliation. In doing so, I attracted more humiliation and pain.

I only realized much later in life that feeling like a victim would make me stay a victim. No one can make us feel anything we do not already feel. We regain power over our lives by taking responsibility for our feelings. Hurt people tend to hurt others. It becomes easier to forgive when you understand this. We can only love others and ourselves unconditionally when we forgive.

SHINE

We all deserve to shine; in fact, it's our duty to shine!

Not long ago, I had a personality test done. One of my traits is that I'm noncompetitive. This wasn't really news to me; winning has never been important to me.

Being noncompetitive is not a negative quality, but it can become one if you give your own wonderful opportunities away to avoid making others feel bad, like I did. I've also discovered that while I am not competitive toward others, I am competitive with myself. This is fine, as long as it improves the self instead of destroying it with burning ambition and an unsatisfiable appetite for success.

We all deserve to shine; in fact, it's our duty to shine!

Many years ago I consulted a life coach to help me understand why I was not excelling in my career the way I thought I should be. I also wanted to learn how to live a life worth living! I have always liked learning as much as I could as fast as I could and researched everything that interested me, so it was only natural for me to research life. I learned that I could avoid a lot of potholes with clear directions, and learning from other people's mistakes provided me with the perfect map. For example, my husband and I once went on a team-building excursion. Tied to a safety harness with ropes above our heads to hold on to for balance, we had to walk across a suspended pole swinging from side to side almost 50 feet above the ground.

The ropes were strategically placed; we had to let go of one rope to reach the next. If we didn't let go, we would inevitably lose our balance and fall. The purpose of the whole exercise was to teach us that you can't go forward until you let go of the past; the very thing you're holding on to will cause you to fall—but they only told us this afterward.

Naturally I chose to tackle the challenge last. I wanted to see what everyone else did before trying it. My darling husband went first. He fell off three times before he made it across; that's the way he likes to do things. After studying his attempts, I felt more confident going up there. Armed with the information I'd gathered and absolute determination to succeed, I managed to walk across the pole on my first attempt; that's the way I like to do things.

You can't go forward if you can't let go of the past; the very thing you're holding on to will cause you to fall.

Now that I've explained to you in my roundabout way why I decided to consult a life coach, let me get back to what that coach, Hanna Kok, taught me. Hanna told me to imagine the entire population of Earth as one body. Every part of this "body" is very important and has its own function.

She then asked me what would happen if the heart decided to beat with less enthusiasm so that the kidneys or liver wouldn't feel unimportant. It would affect the whole body! We all have different special functions in this body that we're part of, and it's vital that we always do our best. If we don't, it has a negative effect on everything and everyone around us.

Having come from a generation where we were taught always to stay in our place, I have been inspired by this quote from Marianne Williamson:

Our deepest fear is not that we are inadequate; our deepest fear is that we are powerful beyond measure. It is our light, not our darkness, that most frightens us. We ask ourselves: Who am I to be brilliant, gorgeous, talented, fabulous? Actually, who are you *not* to be? You are a child of God. Your playing small doesn't serve the world. There's nothing enlightened about shrinking so that other people won't feel insecure around you ... We were born to make manifest the glory of God that is within us. It's not just in some of us, it's in everyone. And as we let our light shine, we unconsciously give other people permission to do the same. As we are liberated from our own fear, our presence automatically liberates others.[1]

With the help of Hanna and many other wise guides, I finally granted myself something I really desired. In 2010, I was chosen to perform with the legendary Italian tenor Andrea Bocelli at the grand finale of "Celebrate Africa," held at the Coca-Cola Dome in Johannesburg in celebration of the FIFA World Cup being hosted in South Africa.

After the performance we were called onto the stage for a final bow. We hadn't rehearsed this, so no one was really sure where to go or what to do. I really wanted to stand next to Andrea Bocelli because he's such an amazing human being, and I wanted this special moment to last a little longer. When we were called, I walked on without hesitation and stood right next to him! Usually I would have fallen back and allowed everyone to walk on before me, but that evening I decided that I also deserved to be there. This was the first time in my 38 years that I granted myself the spotlight, finally allowing myself to shine, humbly and with absolute gratitude.

I'M THERE FOR ME

I can be extremely tough on myself! It's really rather arrogant of me to believe I should do everything perfectly all the time, isn't it? After my husband fell off that pole three times, I couldn't help wondering how that must have felt. He told me afterward that it had been a blast! We filmed the event. Watching him fall was a lot more fun than watching me walk across perfectly.

Bring the fun into your work and work at having fun!

I know he had more fun than I did. He just went for it without thinking about it too much. It was hard work for me because I chose to turn it into work. The secret is to find a healthy balance between work and fun. Bring the fun into your work and work at having fun!

If I had fallen off that day, I would have been very angry with myself. I had such high expectations of myself that it had become very difficult being me. People treat us the way we treat ourselves; on top of it all, people around me started having high expectations, and I had to avoid disappointing them, too! I had complicated my own life so much that I constantly felt angry and frustrated. I used to think I was very forgiving, but then I realized that it's impossible to forgive others if you can't forgive yourself first.

Hanna gave me a very handy technique to help me be more gentle and caring toward myself. She told me to picture myself as a little girl—small and very vulnerable—every time I got angry with myself. I have this picture of myself with

People treat us the way we treat ourselves.

pigtails and freckles taken when I was about seven years old, and every time I see that picture, I feel the urge to protect that little girl. When I'm tough on myself, I think of myself as that little girl; how would she feel if I was that angry with her or treated her that way? I've made that little girl a promise to be there and look out for her no matter what. I will protect her from anger and frustration and anything else that might hurt her, because I love and accept her just the way she is!

WE TEACH WHAT WE NEED TO LEARN

When I was four months pregnant with the girls, my father and I had a huge argument. As I mentioned, I am definitely my father's child. We are both strong-willed, passionate, emotional, and, at times, just downright complicated—but we mean well at heart. After this argument, I took it upon myself to write down a few steps to teach my father how to love himself, as I felt this was his problem. Not long after sending them to him, it dawned on me how funny it was that while trying to teach him, I was struggling with the very same thing!

At times, writing this book has also seemed ironic. I am writing about the very things I struggle with. I guess that's why recovered alcoholics dedicate their lives to helping other alcoholics, or why people who have suffered great loss comfort others who have suffered the same experiences. By doing this, we constantly remind ourselves of what to do in order to continue healing ourselves. I can honestly say that writing this book has felt like nonstop therapy. My dad never mentioned my letter, but after that incident there was a positive change, and today we have the most wonderful relationship. Here's what I wrote to my father and what I still remind myself of every day.

MY GUIDE TO LOVING MYSELF UNCONDITIONALLY:

1. **To love myself is to understand myself:** I know and accept my weaknesses and use them as a guide to better myself. I also know and accept my strengths and continue to develop them.

2. **To love myself is to accept myself:** When I accept myself unconditionally, I find it easier to accept others unconditionally. When I accept others, it becomes easier for them to accept me. By accepting myself, I give myself permission to be who I am.

3. **To love myself is to trust myself:** When I trust myself, I am able to choose what is best for me. It becomes easier to trust others when I trust myself.

4. **To love myself is to have faith in myself:** When I believe in myself, I can make my dreams come true.

5. **To love myself is to forgive myself:** To forgive myself is to admit when I am wrong and to take responsibility. To forgive myself, I must learn from my mistakes and then let them go. When I forgive myself, it becomes easier to forgive others.

6. **To love myself is to be honest with myself:** What I notice in others, I also have in me. The more it bothers me in someone else, the more I need to work on improving that quality in myself.

7. **To love myself is to take responsibility for myself:** I must ensure that I am taking care of myself spiritually, mentally, and physically, and I must also do whatever I can to grow in each of those areas.

8. **To love myself is to find happiness within myself:** My happiness does not depend on others, material possessions, or success; happiness lies within.

9. **To love myself is to be in control of myself:** I must stay in control of my emotions and try not to allow fear, guilt, anger, or any other negative emotion to control me.

10. **To love myself is to enjoy my life:** Enjoy this moment, because this moment is all I have.

11. **To love myself is to attract greatness to myself:** I attract to myself that which I am—not what I want or think. I must be what I desire to attract to myself.

12. **To love myself is to always remember that I am enough:** I accept that nothing else is needed.

CHAPTER TWO

FOLLOWING MY DREAMS AND REACHING MY GOALS

REALITY

R eleasing my first album was one of the biggest challenges I have ever had to face. I just couldn't find a record company willing to release my music! I went from company to company, some of them over and over again. Their answer was almost always the same: "You really sing very nicely, but who will we sell your music to?"

My style of writing is unique, which makes it harder to sell. I had always believed I just needed to be heard by the right people and they would immediately see my potential. The reality was that if I wanted to succeed, I would have to help myself.

At that stage I had recorded all my demos using piano and voice only. I knew that I needed to have my songs arranged and produced to give the record companies a better idea, but this was a very expensive exercise and I could hardly pay my rent.

Once I had to pawn all the jewelry I had received over Christmases and birthdays through the years, only to get 450 rand, which still left me 250 rand short for rent.

When I was little, my parents bought me an endowment policy that matured when I completed my studies. I received enough money to buy myself a small PA system consisting of two speakers, a desk, a power amp, and a microphone. I wouldn't have been able to work without this gear, so I was extremely thankful for it.

The reality was that if I wanted to succeed, I would have to help myself.

I took my CV, plus a demo CD, to every live music venue I could find—both in Johannesburg and Pretoria—to try to find work (or as we say in the music industry, to "find a gig"). I did some one-man-band (or in my case, one-girl-band) shows and also teamed up with other musicians occasionally. I did everything myself—I set up my own instruments and gear before the gig, did my own sound, performed, and then packed everything up after a long night before going home.

I was really strong in those days; I could carry speakers so big that I could hardly fit my arms around them. I used to balance them on my legs and shuffle along, but when I met my husband, he started helping out, and within a month I could no longer lift them!

I performed at weddings, funerals, and private parties, but mostly at pubs and restaurants. I am very sensitive to smoke and suffered badly in the pubs, but did whatever I had to in order to survive and not have to work in an office. At one point I was so poor that a friend offered me a job to help me out. I started early in the morning, filled in all the employment forms, listened to them explaining what I had to do, and quit before lunchtime; I just couldn't see myself doing something I wasn't passionate about—not even for a single day. That reminds me—I never did get paid for those few hours!

I performed at some very interesting places and definitely paid my dues. At one venue the bathroom could only be reached through a *shebeen* (like a speakeasy or juke joint). Needless to say, there weren't many people at that restaurant, and I never went to the bathroom.

One night at a similar place, a man came running into the restaurant shouting, "Fight, fight!" Most of the men jumped up while the women shouted at them to sit down. It was chaos! I just kept on singing the lovely ballad "Tonight, I Celebrate My Love for You."

I didn't enjoy learning new songs—I preferred writing them—so my repertoire wasn't very big. I only had enough songs to make it through a night's performance and never encouraged requests. Often my style of music didn't suit the venue I was playing, and that made my life very complicated. People would continually ask me to sing something nice; I thought I *was* singing something nice, but they were there to party and wanted something with a beat instead of a message.

One night I was singing in a small pub down the road from our house, and my husband came along to support me. Some guys at one of the tables kept shouting, "Smashing Pumpkins! Smashing Pumpkins!" (the popular alternative rock band). I realized they were making fun because it was crazy to request something by Smashing Pumpkins from me, but I was too shy to try to put them in their place. Most of my fellow musicians would have handled them easily by saying something like, "Nice shirt—what did your mom do with the rest of the curtain?"

I was dying a slow death on the stage when my husband walked over to their table and said something to them. They were quiet after that. Later that night I asked him what he had said. He had told them that they should come outside with him if they wanted to hear "smashing pumpkins." My husband, my hero!

Things became worse when I lent my PA system to a fellow musician and never got it back. He left it at the venue where he had performed the previous evening and discovered, when he went to fetch it the next morning, that there had been a break-in during the night and the place had been cleaned out. That was a very expensive lesson, but I am grateful for it today. I've learned that when you've worked hard for something, you appreciate it so much more, and you also look after it better.

Then I landed a great gig playing background music on a lovely grand piano in the lounge area at the Michelangelo Hotel in Sandton, a suburb of Johannesburg. In the beginning I played through the house sound system, but later I saved enough money to buy a small amplifier speaker with a built-in reverb unit. Within two years I was playing at three five-star hotels. Finally, I was managing to pay the bills.

The Hilton was my favorite hotel because the food was so good there! I played on a grand piano that stood near the center of the buffet in the restaurant. I did four sets, each 40 minutes long, and while I played I would plan what I was going to eat during my breaks! Indeed, I ate very well. I also looked well. I was about 30 pounds overweight—but at least my knowledge of food expanded; they served the best of every kind of cuisine you can think of!

Doing background music is very tricky; you can never play quietly enough! Someone will always come and ask you to take the volume down because they can't hear their conversation. Once, someone even asked me if I could perhaps not sing at all—just play the piano.

The great thing about being a background artist is that you can sing anything you like because no one's really listening. I used to make up songs and lyrics as I went along. Sometimes I even sang, "No one's listening to me, I can sing whatever I want."

I loved Chinese audiences; they used to give me one U.S. dollar per request. They obviously loved Bette Midler because they always requested her songs, and afterward the whole family would take a photo with me. They made me feel so famous!

One evening a kind French gentleman bought me a bottle of Dom Pérignon, which cost an arm and a leg at the hotel in those days. When he left, I tried in vain to sell it back to the hotel for cash. Here's some advice: When tipping a starving musician, give them cash instead of expensive gifts; that way they will at least be able to buy bread and milk. Or save up to record a better demo.

We often judge people by what we are thinking and feeling.

I often thought people were irritated by my music. I became very annoyed one night when I noticed the people at a particular table staring at me. I expected them to come and ask me to sing more quietly at any moment—but when they eventually stood up to leave, they all complimented me as they walked past! I felt really embarrassed. I realized something that day: We often judge people by what we are thinking and feeling, but we can't know what others feel unless we are psychic—we can only guess. We should make sure that it's not our ego doing the guesswork.

Singing at hotels was a great platform for practicing my own material, and it allowed me to prepare myself for bigger things. In the beginning I just sang and kept to myself because I was shy and still felt very insecure, but later I realized that I could turn things around for myself by being more open. I started to mingle with the guests during my breaks and met the most interesting people from all over the world. Music brought us together—but I had to open myself up first.

Music is an international language, and that is why I often don't put words to the beautiful melodies that come to me. Instead, I use vocal sounds, leaving space for listeners to interpret the melody for themselves. I call it my "Angel Tongue," because when I sing like that, I am praying for the world and myself to be healed by love.

There are many ways to get to where we want to be . . . we just need to be flexible.

When I learned to look at my hotel audiences through loving eyes, I started to enjoy singing for them and they started to enjoy listening to me.

Very soon I had regulars who became friends and eventually contributed to my career, helping me financially and teaching me about business.

Some of them were well-established businesspeople, and I learned a great deal from them! One of the things I learned was that when you're young and climbing the ladder, your only focus is reaching the top. Once you've landed there, a new desire fills your heart: the desire to help others reach the top as well. I understood this and accepted their help gratefully, knowing that I would do the same one day. I will remain forever thankful for their generosity and kindness, but mostly for the fact that they believed in me.

I have to mention my very dear Irish friend, Victor Richards, because it was with his help that I managed to record my first album. Victor taught me a very important lesson: There are many ways to get to where you want to be … you just need to be flexible.

At that stage I was as rigid as a pole in my thinking, and if I had kept that stubborn attitude, I would still be playing in a lounge somewhere. I had to learn to be open to new ideas and to do things differently. This was challenging, but with the help of many wise and patient teachers I eventually managed to succeed.

Finally I had a complete album and a record company showing some interest! They offered me a recording deal, but my lawyer advised me strongly against signing it. The deal wasn't a good one and would have harmed my career in the long run. Imagine the disappointment of finally receiving an offer, having to turn it down, and then having to spend the next three years paying the lawyer's fee—still with NO DEAL!

I believe books come to me at the right time; I take from them whatever resonates for me and leave the rest.

By the time I was 28 (which is considered old in the music industry), I was depressed and miserable. Nothing seemed to be going my way. I felt like the world was out to get me, and life was bleak and painful for me.

There was no way I could stay healthy with that many negative feelings, and I soon became very ill. It was a terrible time for me. After being sick at home for weeks, I was finally admitted to the hospital. My blood tests revealed a virus, but the doctors couldn't determine what kind.

On the second day they took a urine sample, and the next minute they were injecting insulin into my stomach—the urine test had shown that I was diabetic. In the end, it turned out that I wasn't diabetic at all; my system was just severely run-down. I had such a scare! I promised myself that I would never allow myself to become that ill again. Since then I have had minor illnesses, but never anything that severe.

Then someone gave me an amazing book called *Conversations with God*[1] by Neale Donald Walsch, and parts of what it said changed my life! I believe books come to me at the right time; I take from them whatever resonates for me and leave the rest. You should keep that in mind while reading this book.

> *Success is simply doing what you love.*

I came to realize that I was already a success story! I had a wonderful man in my life, I was healthy, I had a roof over my head and food to eat, and on top of everything, I was doing what I loved—singing. It's strange how we think success means having wealth, security, and fame. The truth is that success is simply doing what you love.

The minute I *felt* successful, more success came my way. That's just the way life works. We attract what we are and what we feel about ourselves.

WHO PAINTED THE MOON?

Just before I turned 30, my music landed in the hands of Benjy Mudie, owner of Fresh Music, a small independent record company in South Africa. Thirty, by the way, is the cutoff age for entering the popular South African reality TV show *Idols*—not that I have ever been interested in entering; I just want to emphasize that the music industry doesn't think artists can still make it after 30.

I signed a deal with Fresh Music, and my first album, *Who Painted the Moon?*, was released in October 2001. I wrote the title song one night in February 2001 after my husband called me while I was working at the Hilton and told me to look outside; there was something amazing I had to see.

> *The magic of songs and also of life lies in simplicity.*

I went out and saw the most beautiful lunar eclipse just above me. It felt so close that I was incredibly moved by it. Looking at the moon that night, I prayed for something special to happen—and something special did happen. I kept looking at the moon through my car window as I drove home after my gig, and the melody and words just poured out of me.

The song was almost complete when I arrived at home 20 minutes later. I went straight to the piano and finished it within an hour. At first I thought it was too simple and I was reluctant to put it on my first album, but my husband and Benjy persuaded me that it had hit potential and that I should name the album after it. I took their advice, and when the song did become a hit, I realized something very important: The magic of songs—and also of life—lies in simplicity.

WHO PAINTED THE MOON?

Did you see the shiny moon
Turned into a black balloon
Just as you walked away from me?

Did you see how hard I've tried
Not to show the pain inside
Just as you walked away from me?

Who painted the moon black
Just when you asked your love back?
Who painted the moon black?
Oh won't you, won't you come back?
Who painted the moon?

It must have been the darkest night,
Not even a star in sight
Just as you walked away from me.

Who painted the moon black
Just when you asked your love back?
Who painted the moon black?
Oh won't you, won't you come back?
Who painted the moon?

Did you see the shiny moon
Turned into a black balloon
Just as you walked away from me?
Who painted the moon black

Just when you've asked your love back?
Who painted the moon black?
Oh won't you, won't you come back?
Who painted the moon?

Before my album was released, my husband took it to Highveld Stereo (a radio station), and they immediately started playing my song "Have Faith."

One night they invited people to phone in and vote for their favorite local artist. I figured I had better vote for myself in case no one else did and used my husband's phone to send an SMS. Imagine his embarrassment when they phoned him the next day, congratulating him on winning a radio and thanking him for his vote! We still have that radio, just for luck.

Later on, "Just for Tonight," "Isn't It?" and "Who Painted the Moon?" also received great radio exposure, not just locally, but also internationally. "Isn't It?" did particularly well; I still remember the night it came to me. It was around two in the morning, and I needed some serious motivation.

ISN'T IT?

Isn't it strange the way we hide behind our fears?
Isn't it strange how many times we change our minds?
Isn't it comfortable to never make a stand?
Isn't it comfortable to blend in with the crowd?

If you know it's inside of you,
Why not believe in what you can do?
Do you know you can change the way things are?
If you see it, you can be it

Isn't it funny how we always play pretend?
Isn't it funny how we try to fool the world?
Isn't it typical to blame someone else?
Isn't it typical to make a lame excuse?
If you know it's inside of you,
Why not believe in what you can do?

Do you know you can change the way things are?
If you see it, you can be it

Breaking the silence, could it change the way we think?
Changing the way we think, isn't it the link?

Believe in what you can do, you can change . . .

Even though my music was receiving great radio exposure, I sold very few CDs. Releasing a CD doesn't guarantee sales! The only thing you've done is to step onto the field; now you have to get out there and score a goal! That takes time, hard work, and determination. You don't just walk into the position of CEO after high school graduation! I've learned that "overnight success" takes about 15 years.

The album was moving slowly, so I decided to cash in an endowment I had taken out for myself years before. I used the money to go to KKNK—the Klein Karoo Arts Festival, which is held in Oudtshoorn (in South Africa's Western Cape province) once a year. I performed on all the open stages for free, just to get some exposure. I managed to do one personal show, but only seven people came. I still feel relieved when people come to my shows, and I remain thankful for every seat that's filled.

After the festival we drove to Cape Town, where I had pre-arranged another four shows in theaters and restaurants. I worked hard to fill the venues, handing out flyers and putting up posters everywhere. In the next month my CD sales increased to 3,000. I realized then just how important it was to perform. Selling CDs requires a combination of radio, TV, and other media exposure, but live performances are essential.

Then suddenly Universal Records UK took interest in my music. They were in South Africa at the time, and Benjy arranged an audition for me. I blew them away! They were so impressed that they offered me a deal and spoke about giving me almost 3 million rand in advance. The deal was never presented on paper, but we were very excited and even started looking at properties; we had big plans and already felt rich.

One night I was sitting in the bath thinking about the money that was coming my way and suddenly caught myself having selfish thoughts—about money I hadn't even received yet. I didn't like my head space and thought that it would be better not to get the money if it was going to make me so self-absorbed. I don't know whether I jinxed it or whether it was just not meant to be, but shortly after that, Universal Records went through some major changes and had to cut many of their existing artists. My deal didn't go through.

I don't regret it—things always happen exactly as they should. What I did learn was never to count my chickens before they've hatched. We give money strange powers; I think it's healthier to become used to it in small amounts and let it grow slowly. That way you can grow with it and remain appreciative. I can completely understand when I hear that someone has allowed money to change them, or that people who have won the lottery are broke again within months. Fame can have the same effect.

ANGEL TONGUE

I invested almost all the money I made from live performances and CD sales back into recording and marketing my second album. My policy is "It's all right to receive help once, but after that you need to help yourself." Sometimes you just need a little push to start things rolling, but after that, it's crucial to keep the momentum going with your own efforts.

After my first album I financed all my own CDs. This meant that I owned the rights to my music and had final say in my projects, which is the way I prefer it. I am grateful that things worked out this way. If, years ago, I had struck a deal right away, I would not have owned the rights to my music. I also wouldn't have known the ins and outs of the music industry the way I do now. Walking the long road definitely held more advantages for me.

It's all right to receive help once, but after that you need to help yourself.

Benjy sent my first album to a publishing contact of his in London, and they immediately managed to place "Who Painted the Moon?" onto up-and-coming New Zealand artist Hayley Westenra's album *Pure*, which became a smash hit, selling more than 2.5 million copies worldwide. My song was featured on her album as a single.

This was something I had never anticipated, and it changed my focus slightly in that I was now trying to place more of my songs with international artists. I didn't think of my music as "just music"—it was music with a message of love.

Since I was a little girl I have loved inspiring and motivating people, and I believe this is my true calling. Music is my medium, and I thought the message would spread much faster if more people like Hayley could sing my songs.

With my second album I tried to capture as many different styles of music as I could in the hope that more international artists might cover my songs. I included songs like "Monday," a blues song that I composed when I was introduced to the blues in my first year of studying music and just loved it. I also included the classical "It's So Absurd," an almost hip-hop–style song called "Life," and a country song called "Slowly Killing Me," so as you can see, there was a big variety.

I called the album *Angel Tongue,* and it did very well in southern Africa. I won two SAMA (South African Music Awards) awards with it: Best Female Composer of the Year for "We'll Find a Way" and Best English Adult Contemporary Album of the Year. I wasn't even there to receive them! I had committed to another performance long before the SAMAs were scheduled, and it would not have been right to cancel. To be honest I didn't even think of canceling because I hadn't realized I would win anything. It was a wonderful surprise when I did!

Whatever happens is what's meant to be.

My endeavor to place more songs with international artists has not paid off yet, but I am at peace with whatever happens. By now I have taught myself to be patient. Through the years I have learned that I can't rush things.

My climb was slow because I needed to learn so much along the way, and I am still learning every day. Whatever happens is what's meant to be. I still have big dreams, though, and one of my dreams is that my song "We'll Find a Way" will find its way into a Disney movie. I am a huge Disney fan, and when I wrote this song in the early hours of the morning, I was totally lost in the fantasy of an animated movie.

WE'LL FIND A WAY

Close your eyes, my love
Imagine flying high above
Where we can feel the magic
Of the stars surrounding us
Where we can be
Almost anything we want to be
Just you and me, my love, you'll see,
We'll find a way

Don't hide away, my love, you'll see,
We'll find a way

Hold on to our dreams,
No matter how, how far it seems
Remember us,
Always and forever like we're now
And in my heart,
You'll know we'll never be apart
Just you and me, my love, you'll see,
We'll find a way

Don't hide away, my love, you'll see,
We'll find a way

LIFE'S GIFT

Life's Gift, my third and favorite album, was released in 2005 by Sony Music Africa. After the success of my first two albums, *Who Painted the Moon?* and *Angel Tongue,* I found myself in a better position to negotiate a good deal with a major record company. Benjy Mudie from Fresh Music was kind enough to release me from our contract; we both knew that it would be better for my career if I moved to a bigger international company. Benjy remains one of my most trusted advisers, and I never enter into an agreement without his valuable input.

I knew what I wanted from Sony Music, and I was ready to negotiate a great recording deal with them. I remember sitting in their boardroom with all their executives, discussing and reviewing every option. Like any good businessman would have done, the CEO, whom I liked very much and still do, was trying to convince me to give them the rights to my previous two albums as well.

Listening is one of the most vital skills—both in business and in life.

This was something I was not prepared to do. I am telling you this story because on that day, I learned that listening is one of the most vital skills—both in business and in life; thank goodness I was doing just that at the time. As I was saying, the CEO was stating his case and I was listening.

I have never met a more convincing person in my life! He was mesmerizing as he presented the facts while drawing pictures on a big white sheet of paper. Did I mention he was a qualified lawyer? Halfway through his presentation I suddenly realized that he had already convinced me.

It was a good thing that I carried on listening instead of saying aloud what I was thinking. That's the power of listening. You buy yourself a few chances to come to your senses if you listen well for long enough. As I realized that I had been convinced, I suddenly saw three paths in front of me: to surrender and give them what they wanted, to fight for what I wanted, or to withdraw. The first path wasn't an option for me, and I have learned from experience that fighting just creates more fighting, so I decided to withdraw—but that meant that I could lose what I wanted.

Life is all about choices and we need to make those choices fearlessly.

Then it hit me! I needed to negotiate fearlessly as though I had nothing to lose, and that's what I did! I told them that I was there to negotiate my future albums, not my previous ones, and also said that all the talk about my past two albums was making me feel very uncomfortable. Everyone got the message loud and clear. Within seconds we were discussing my next album.

I know it could have gone the other way—we might all have dispersed in a matter of seconds—but I was willing to live with the consequences. In that moment I realized yet again that life is all about choices, and we need to make those choices fearlessly. Whatever we choose will take us in a certain direction, and we can change that direction whenever we like. In the end, the path we choose does not matter because there are amazing lessons and experiences on every chosen path.

With every one of my albums I have grown as a musician, but more than that, I have grown spiritually. *Life's Gift* is my favorite album because of the title song. Every time I sing it, I remember that I am merely a vessel!

In the end, the path we choose does not matter because there are amazing lessons and experiences on every chosen path.

How else would it be possible for me to write down wisdom I don't yet comprehend? I still need to apply the knowledge captured in those lyrics to my own life. Five years later, I am still struggling to let go and just be, but because of the blessing of this song, at least I am aware of this.

> *It's when we let go and take a step back to just breathe that things happen the way they should.*

It's when we let go and take a step back to just breathe that things happen the way they should. Our purpose here is to BE. We are, after all, human BEINGS, not human DOINGS. It was always intended that we should *be* happy, *be* fulfilled, *be* in the now, *be* loved, and *be* alive, but we complicated that for ourselves. It seemed too simple; surely it couldn't be that simple, could it? So what did we do? We made it harder for ourselves by thinking we should *do* something to deserve all those gifts. We always want to be in control, and the more we want to be in control, the more out of control we feel.

Looking back, I know this song came to prepare me for the birth of my triplet girls. I always joke that control freaks end up having triplets so that they learn they never have been, and never really will be, in control. All in all, my girls and this song have been a wonderful blessing in my life. Letting go has become a little easier now.

LIFE'S GIFT

High on the wings of an angel I fly,
Light without care without questioning why.
Slowly the night seems to fade into grey.
Day came in time to break my fall

Now I'm awake, I can finally see.
Life's gift to me is just to be...

High on the wings of an angel I fly.
Small is the world from up here in the sky.
Small all my fears and how precious the years,
I can hardly see the tears from here.

Now that I know I am finally free
Life's gift to me is just to be...
I've been trying to please
Always longing to ease,

NIANELL
Life's Gift

Wondering just what it is,
Guess I already know,
Nothing I do will make it so

I'm letting go, letting go faithfully.
Life's gift to me is just to be...

AS ONE

It was time to bring out a DVD; I called it *As One*. It was a live performance of songs from my first three albums joined into one show. "As One" is also the title of one of the songs on my first album. Although we are all uniquely different, we are at the same time very similar. I believe we are all one, and I would love to see the world unite as one. I believe music has the power to achieve this. Can you imagine a world anthem sung by everyone on the planet at exactly the same time? "As One" is my anthem.

Here is a perfect example of where I've used vocal sounds instead of words with the melody that came to me. In doing so, I try not to take away from what the music might evoke in each individual, leaving the space for the listener to interpret it.

AS ONE

Ha ha ha, omde, shodode,
Omdaje, ehije, ohije,
Mohija, shedade

I've heard an angel's voice,
Leaving me no choice.
Say it loud and clear,
Everyone must hear.

Break the chains of silence.
Break the bonds of hate.
Everyone must sing.
Everyone must feel.

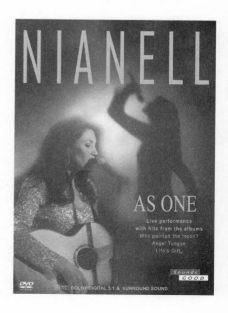

Feel the music slowly taking control.
Feel the rhythm breathing through your soul.
You know the time has come,
For music to join us as one

Ha ha ha, omde, shodode (Be together as one)
Omdaje, ehije, ohije,
Mohija, shedade

Raise your voice in love.
Raise your voice in hope.
Everyone must sing.
Everyone must feel

Feel the music slowly taking control.
Feel the rhythm breathing through your soul.
You know the time has come,
For music to join us as one

Ha ha ha, omde, shodode (Be together as one)
Omdaje, ehije, ohije,
Mohija, shedade

Ha ha ha, omde, shodode,
Omdaje, ehije,
Ohija, shedade

I gave birth to our girls about a year after the release of this DVD. My husband and I funded the project ourselves, so we were thankful that it was successful. I had to take some time off during my pregnancy, and the income from the DVD helped to sustain us for a while.

I KNOW I'M LUCKY

The fact that my fourth album, *I Know I'm Lucky,* was ever written and completed is a miracle. It was put together during a crazy time in our lives. Most of the songs were written just before and during my pregnancy, and the album was recorded shortly after the girls were born. To this day I still don't know how we managed to do it—exhaustion can make you forget things—but we needed to keep my profile up, so it was vital to bring this album out.

My husband and I decided to join forces in my music career when we fell pregnant with the girls. We felt it would be best for all of us if we worked together so that we would be able to spend more time together, which is very important to us. Working together also meant that there was now one income, and that needed to continue coming in, so we couldn't slack off on releasing albums and doing performances. I started giving live performances again two months after our girls were born.

Your focus changes when you become a mother.

I remember having to express milk for my girls while performing at Skouspel, a big annual Afrikaans music event, in 2007. It really keeps your feet on the ground when you find yourself sitting in a small bathroom, all made up with your ball gown on and a pump connected to your breast, and all you can think about are the three little babies depending on you to provide. Before that, I used to spend hours preparing for the stage! It's funny how your focus changes when you become a mother—as one of my video directors once said, "There's nothing like a dirty nappy to put life into perspective."

I love telling the story of how I was inspired to write "*Sy Word Onthou*" ("She's Being Remembered"), one of the songs on *I Know I'm Lucky*. It all started when I went to the town of Darling to purchase a pregnancy test. We own a house in Yzerfontein on the West Coast, which is a fishing village so small that if you need to go to a pharmacy, you have to drive about 12 miles inland to Darling. I love the West Coast people; they have an amazing sense of humor and the ability to lift any spirit. That day I gave a ride to three ladies who were employed as domestic workers in Yzerfontein but lived in Darling.

When we got to Darling, I decided to treat them to some groceries. They were absolutely delighted and thanked me in typical West Coast style! "*O, die Here sal jou seen!*" ("The Lord will bless you!"). I told them to get what they needed while

I quickly popped into the pharmacy to buy not one, but three pregnancy tests, just to be sure. When I came back, I saw them standing outside with their grocery bags, which I realized were going to be very difficult for them to carry, so I offered to take them home.

Two of the ladies stayed just outside Darling, but the third told me she "stayed far." I said that was okay, but realized later that she had been very serious about that. We got to know each other pretty well during that trip, and when we finally arrived at the farm where she was staying, she told me, "The road ends here; we'll have to walk the rest of the way."

We climbed out of the car and started carrying the groceries up a hill when she turned to me and said, "*Stap sy nou op 'n plaaspad met die groceries in 'n sak*," which basically means, "I can't believe that I'm seeing *you* on a farm road with a bag of groceries." I loved the way she put that and decided to use the line in a song.

> *You realize just how much you have when you give.*

The first thing I did when I got home that night was to find out if I was pregnant. All three tests came up positive, and again I just marveled at the fact that you realize just how much you have when you give. The second thing I did was to capture the memory of my lovely day in song.

"Down in Dew" is another special song on this album. My husband and I wrote the lyrics together, and it tells the story of our life together so far. "Dew" is short for Honeydew—the Johannesburg suburb where we met. I was performing in a pub called "Duck and Dive" (can you believe it?), and it really was a dive! I don't know what his excuse for hanging out there was. How do you tell people you met your husband in a pub called "Duck and Dive"? In a song, of course!

Many years of experience had taught me that men didn't approach me or ask me out, so if I wanted to meet someone, I had to make the first move. When I saw Andrew across the crowded room, I decided to send him my business card. A whole week went by before he called me, and today he always jokes that it took him a week to work through all the business cards he received that night. The song covers three stages of our lives and was also written in three stages over a period of time: when and how we met, how we've grown and settled in, and a final verse about our girls, written after their birth.

DOWN IN DEW

I met you downtown in Dew
The place was old, my songs were new.
You didn't notice me at all
I sent a note and hoped you'd call.
A cracked-up junkie ran the bar,
I knew 'round here I won't get far.
But we had time and we were young
And that is how it all begun

The years flew by, still we go on
And now the place in Dew is gone.
Our dogs are old, this house is new
And I'm still crazy over you.
And on the radio plays a tune.
I wrote it way back in June
When I was playing down in Dew
That was the place where I met you

Time will tell the story well
And that is all I need to know
What I have is here and now
And now is all I'm living for

Last Christmas it was you and me
Now we're an instant family
There's hardly space under our tree
Instead of one we were blessed with three
Yes, life's been good to us so far
To think it started in a bar
Do you remember down in Dew
That was the place where I met you

Time will tell the story well
And that is all I need to know
What I have is here and now
And now is all I'm living for

I've met you downtown in Dew
The place was old, my songs were new.
You didn't notice me at all
I sent a note and hoped you'd call.
A cracked-up junkie ran the bar,
I knew 'round here I won't get far.
But we had time and we were young
And that is how it all begun

As I mentioned earlier, I wrote the title track of this album, "I Know I'm Lucky," before I found out I was pregnant.

The piano part for this song is very tricky, and I sang the title over and over to get it just right. Today I am a firm believer in positive affirmations!

I KNOW I'M LUCKY

Today I took some time to think about life
To take a look at all the struggle and strife
And as I recall all the years that's gone by
I could see that I was up more than down

I know I'm lucky
I have it all
I find my freedom in loving you, loving life
Loving you, loving life

I used to only see all that I'm not
Instead of noticing the treasures I've got
Working on ways to get out in front
Until it hit me you've got to be what you want

I know I'm lucky

I have it all

I find my freedom in loving you, loving life

Loving you, loving life

And as the morning light shines down on me

I pull the covers back, I'm happy as can be

Because in the midst of all the answers I seek

I finally realized I've been looking too deep

SAND & WATER

My first three albums did very well, and I had even higher expectations for *I Know I'm Lucky*. Although this album did reach gold status, my expectations for it were much higher and I felt very disappointed when it did not meet them. I started to question my songwriting abilities, and before I knew it, I had lost faith in what I was doing. I fell back into my old negative way of thinking. People didn't want to hear my style of music. It was too complicated. *I* was too complicated.

I doubted my talent, my abilities, and even my purpose. It wasn't a very good place to be, especially since I needed to start working on my next album. I put the word out among my songwriting friends that I was looking for good songs. Even writing this now makes me want to blush. It was like an artist asking his friends to finish his painting, his work of art. What was I thinking?! I'm sure the end result would have been great, but it would not have fulfilled my purpose. I needed to learn that what I create is perfect as it is, whether it's in demand or not.

One of my supporters made me aware of this one evening when she sent an e-mail requesting that I perform one of the songs off *Life's Gift*.

The song was "Crazy about My Life." I hadn't done it for a while, so just to refresh my memory I

I make music not only to sell CDs and earn money, but because it's my passion and my life's purpose.

decided to listen to it on the way to the performance. I hardly ever listen to my own CDs, but I continued to listen to the whole album on my way home that evening, and an incredible peace came over me. Every song spoke to me, reminding me of my purpose. By the time I arrived, I believed in myself again and remembered why I make music: not only to sell CDs and earn money, but because it's my passion and my life's purpose.

CRAZY ABOUT MY LIFE

My head is up in the clouds
I don't know much about much
I just know I'm crazy about my life

I'm slightly off in a crowd
I don't really go with the flow
I just like to take things kind of slow

I don't give up in a hurry
Nothing you do makes me worry
I take control of the way things go

I wake up late in the mornings
Nothing I do's ever boring
And if it is I'll just change my ways

I try to smell the roses everywhere I go
And if it rains I know a rainbow's going to show

If it's the darkest night I wish upon a star
If it's the end I had the greatest ride by far
I say hey

My head is up in the clouds
I don't know much about much
I just know I'm crazy about my life

I showed my fear the way out
I told it to never come back
I walked it all the way out that door
Some people live for the moment
And others plan it forever
I took that moment and made it mine
So come and dance with me, baby
Don't let me hear you say maybe
For this may be all we ever have

Embrace the pleasure of being
Entice the nothing we're seeing
And that's to sum up all I know

I try to smell the roses everywhere I go
And if it rains I know a rainbow's going to show

If it's the darkest night I wish upon a star
If it's the end I had the greatest ride by far
I say hey

My head is up in the clouds
I don't know much about much
I just know I'm crazy about my life

My album *Sand & Water* came to life during a time of doubt, but it carried me toward solid ground, and now I know for certain why I have to write and sing the songs that come to me. Thanks to my growth during the making of this album, I am now at peace with the music that comes to me.

I embrace the uniqueness of every song and understand what its purpose is: It is meant to heal and teach. If my songs become hits, that is merely a bonus.

The song "Sand & Water" is the only song on this album that I did not write. It was composed by my idol, Beth Nielson Chapman (who also wrote the song "This Kiss," sung by Faith Hill). I was introduced to Beth's music about eight years ago

I believe the ability to feel music by listening to it is just as big a talent as being able to make and compose music.

when a friend gave me a compilation CD for my birthday. I will never forget the day I first listened to it. We were driving somewhere and when "Sand & Water" came on, everything stopped for me.

Beth's husband had died of cancer, and she wrote this song in his memory. The hook line is "Solid stone is just sand and water and a million years gone by." Beth has an incredible way with words that touches my soul deeply.

I believe that the ability to feel music by listening to it is just as big a talent as being able to make music. I haven't been blessed with the "feeling" gift. I have to make music to feel it through an audience—but when "Sand & Water" started playing that day, I felt it. I picked up the CD cover to find out who had written the song and made a point of memorizing her name.

About three years later I was in studio with an amazing producer who told me he would soon be going to Nashville and planned to stay with his good friend Beth Nielson Chapman. I nearly fell off my chair. He gave me all her CDs to listen to, and I gave him mine to give to her. Not long after that, Beth came to visit South Africa and I had the wonderful privilege of meeting her. She's a wonderful, warm person, but what I am most thankful for is the fact that she helped me experience being in the audience's shoes—being able to feel the music without having to perform it myself.

We have it all in the palms of our hands— everything we need to make this life a success.

Beth was kind enough to allow me to sing her song on my album, and we also decided to call the album *Sand & Water,* which read the same way in English and in Afrikaans; a perfect fit for a double CD, one in English and one in Afrikaans.

The song that stands out most for me on the English side of this album is "I Hold the Sun." I was walking on the beach in Yzerfontein one evening and saw the most amazing sunset on my right. The full moon was hanging just above a cliff to my left, and I stretched my hands out to balance the sun and the moon. As I stood there, arms stretched out, looking as if I was holding the sun and moon in my hands, I realized something: We have it all in the palms of our hands; God has given us everything we need to make this life a success. We just need to take hold of it and believe in the abilities we have received from Him.

I HOLD THE SUN

I hold the sun and the moon in my hands
Life has invited me, I want to dance
This is the moment I'm taking a chance
I hold the sun and the moon in my hands

There's nothing to lose
So what if I bruise
Life is what I choose
I've got nothing to lose
I'll find a way

I don't care what they say
I just need a moment, a second, to show who I am
And why I am here
We took what is simple and made it unbelievable
When the answer is that

I hold the sun and the moon in my hands
Life has invited me, I want to dance
This is the moment I'm taking a chance
I hold the sun and the moon in my hands

It's hard to believe
Even harder to achieve
But it's the air that I breathe
Why's it hard to believe
I'll find a way

I don't care what they say
I just need a moment, a second, to show who I am
And why I am here
We took what is simple and made it unbelievable
When the answer is that

I hold the sun and the moon in my hands
Life has invited me, I want to dance
This is the moment, I'm taking a chance
I hold the sun and the moon in my hands

It's all in my hands, I'm taking a chance
I've been waiting too long
For someone else to sing this song

I hold the sun and the moon in my hands
Life has invited me, I want to dance
This is the moment I'm taking a chance
I hold the sun and the moon in my hands

The simple truth is
Yes, the simple truth is
That I hold the sun and the moon in my hands

IT TAKES TWO

After *I Know I'm Lucky*, my husband suggested that I record an album with Dozi, another well-known South African artist. I immediately said no; I couldn't imagine our very different styles working together. I was also still struggling to move out of my comfort zone. Then it was suggested we do a concept album consisting of hit

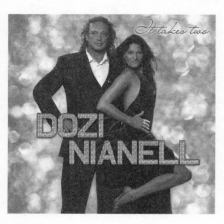

duets from the last two decades, and I fell in love with the idea. I have always admired Dozi's voice and once again discovered how amazing it can be to try something new.

So often when I frown on an idea in the beginning, it turns out to be amazing. Working on well-known songs that we both liked very much helped me tremendously when it came to writing new songs for my next album, and also brought out different elements of my voice and stage personality.

After being a solo artist for so long, it was also a new experience to share the stage with another front artist, and I must say it's a lot more fun having a partner in crime. Singing well-known songs with someone else is not easy—especially if you both struggle to remember words. I never used to forget my words, but having triplets takes a lot out of you. I love singing my own songs because I can just make up new words if I forget, but that is not the case with well-known songs. Dozi and I, however, do attempt it every now and again. We just try to do it with so much confidence that no one will pick up on it—and if they do, we hope that our confidence will make them doubt themselves.

The duet project stretched both of us. We also worked with a choreographer; neither of us is a dancer, but putting in small choreographed movements here and there gave the show a nice

People listen with their eyes.

edge. After that, I had more confidence to move around during my own shows and also became comfortable wearing sexier outfits, whereas before, I had focused only on the music—what I wore hadn't mattered to me, as long as I felt comfortable in it. Doing a Broadway-esque production bought out the actress in me, and I realized there was more to shows than just music—people listen with their eyes.

SAND & WATER DVD

I felt that I had grown considerably as a performer through the years, and I really wanted to capture that on a DVD. Sony Music Africa agreed to fund the project, and I am very thankful for that. This time I included material from all my previous albums, and it was awesome to look back and take notes.

It started with *Who Painted the Moon?*, which was symbolic of that dark and emotional time in my life, then I swooped up to new heights with my album *Angel Tongue*. *Life's Gift* turned me inward, and gratitude came with *I Know I'm Lucky*. I finally found peace with *Sand & Water*.

ENCORE

All we have is now, this moment, and it is my intention to make the best of it, to savor it, to drink it in, and to enjoy it.

All we have is now, this moment, and it is my intention to make the best of it, to savor it, to drink it in, and to enjoy it. I had a dream to love and heal through music. Now I am thankful that I have received love and healing through music and the blessing of living my dream. In the beginning my goal was to become a superstar; now I know that I only have to do what's in front of me and that is enough—the rest will follow.

CHAPTER THREE

BODY, MIND, AND SOUL

I am not my body, nor am I how I look or what I am capable of physically.
I am not my mind, nor am I what I think, feel, or create.
I am not what I can do or what I do.
I am now free to be.

A s human beings, we have a body, a mind, and a soul. Our bodies and minds house the soul for the duration of our stay here. These three work together as a unit to assist us in "being." Our soul guides us, using the body and mind to communicate with us. In order to guide us competently, our soul needs to stay connected to our Creator. Our bodies and minds are precious gifts, given to help us on our journey. It is our responsibility to take care of them and vital to understand that they were given to us for a very specific reason, so we should accept them thankfully. They will help us remember who we are if we allow them to. How we receive them, use them, or abuse them is up to us, but if we do not take care of them, our journey here can become very uncomfortable.

MY BODY

I have had a very interesting relationship with my body. Through the years, I have learned to be more gentle, caring, and understanding toward it. I don't always succeed, but I try, and I have to forgive myself when I fail—if I don't, my body will end up taking the punishment on my behalf.

Being a woman used to be a big challenge for me. Women's bodies change all the time, and I don't like change. When my sister and I reached our teens and our breasts started to develop, we were horrified. We tried everything to stop the growth! We tried to flatten them with tight bandages and even hit them hard just to make them go away, but nothing helped. All this "woman stuff" was too much for me. I found it restrictive and pointless, but there was nothing I could do to make it stop, so I surrendered to it at some point. It's not that I wanted to be a man; I just didn't like all the changes.

To embrace change is to embrace life. Everything changes constantly, and the sooner we accept change, the better life becomes. Years later I actually became immensely grateful for the fact that I am a woman, and embraced my femininity completely.

> *To embrace change is to embrace life.*

Another challenge was staying in shape and maintaining my goal weight. I have always enjoyed being active, so staying fit was never a problem, but my eating habits were—I love food! There's nothing wrong with loving food, but when we use it to reward, compensate, or comfort ourselves, it isn't good for our bodies—and our bodies will let us know it. Mine showed me that it was taking strain; I weighed about 30 pounds more than I should have, and felt it everywhere; not just in my clothes, but also in my back. When my back pain became worse, I finally went to see a chiropractor, who diagnosed me with grade-two spondylolisthesis and strongly suggested that I lose weight to relieve the pressure on my spine, which would reduce the pain. He also referred me to an amazing physical trainer.

Now I have never been on a diet; it's just too hard. Even thinking of going on a diet makes me want to eat more. The closest I have ever come to dieting was a 21-day habit-breaking spree to stop eating after seven at night. This is a very good way to break bad habits, but I suggest you do it with a friend—it really helps to have someone else's support, and not letting one another down is a great motivator.

I went to see a plastic surgeon, thinking I could maybe have some of the fat cut away. I remember standing in his office on a little stepstool in front of a mirror under a very bright lamp that really put the spotlight on all my imperfections. He pointed out areas that we would be able to work on and asked me if I could see all the cellulite. I felt like saying, "I'm fat, not blind!" I guess he sensed my dismay and quickly explained that he'd had to point it out, since the surgery wouldn't remove it. He also explained that after surgery, patients who haven't looked at themselves properly often complain about things they never noticed before. He went on to say that the surgery would be more effective if I reached my goal weight first, which made me wonder, *What's the point of the surgery, then?*

That appointment was a turning point for me. I decided there and then that I was going to lose my extra weight the natural way—by following a healthy lifestyle—not by going on a grueling diet, taking pills, or being cruel to my body in any way. I went to see a dietitian, and her advice—together with the progress I made with my life coach in accepting and loving myself, and training with my physical trainer—helped me reach my goal weight.

The above three go hand in hand, but loving and accepting yourself is by far the most important thing—even if you do reach your goal weight, you won't be happy without this. The best and only diet is loving and accepting yourself; then you will naturally do what's best for your body.

The best and only diet is loving and accepting yourself; then you will naturally do what's best for your body.

I managed to reach my goal weight about a year before I fell pregnant, and this helped me get back in shape much faster afterward. I continued to eat healthfully during my pregnancy and carried on training until about a month before I had my girls. During the last month, I could only do very light stretching exercises and breathing, but it was good to do something. I was fortunate only to gain about 20 pounds instead of the 75 pounds my doctor said I might. Toward the end of my pregnancy, I started losing weight instead of gaining it, and had to take a supplement. I think the girls took a lot out of my body; even my bone structure felt smaller afterward.

It took me a long time to gather the courage to become pregnant. A week after going off the pill, I was so scared that I almost started taking it again; but something told me that if I did, I would miss out on the most amazing experience of my life, so I tried to let go of my fear, and I persisted. One month later I was pregnant with triplets.

At four months I had to have special stitches put in to support the weight my womb was carrying. The next day I flew to Durban to do a show there. I had the worst headache and remember lying down on two hard little chairs to try to relieve it after the show. I had to work for as long as I could and generate as much income as possible; taking care of three little babies was going to be costly.

One performance I will never forget was the one at Loftus Versfeld, a popular sports stadium in Pretoria, where I performed along with several other well-known

South African artists in front of about 25,000 people; it was amazing to have my three little girls on stage with me that day! At five and a half months, I was admitted to the hospital with a bladder infection, and the doctor instructed me to take it easy from then on. I had to cancel about seven performances and stay at home.

Pulanie Naudé

After that, I received regular cortisone injections so that the girls' lungs could develop more quickly. These made me feel dizzy, even though our doctor said they shouldn't have that effect. One day, I went outside to play with my dogs, and as I was picking up a garden chair to sit on, I twisted my ankle and fell. The chair somehow landed upside down with me on top of it. I was home alone and didn't expect my husband back till much later … we had been renting a small place down the road from us while we did some renovations, and he was overseeing the builders.

Too scared to move, I just lay on the grass, praying that the babies would be okay and for Andrew to come home. He arrived ten minutes later, saying that he had just had a feeling! We went straight to the hospital. They knew us there since I had been going for regular ultrasounds and checkups. Thankfully the girls were alive, but it was hard to tell if they were all right because they didn't move around a lot—I guess there wasn't enough space. We had such a scare!

I gave birth about a month later, at 33 weeks, on July 30, 2007. Our doctor decided it would be safer to avoid natural labor, which would have been very risky since I had never given birth before. I spent the weekend in the hospital and had a cesarean at eight o'clock on that Monday morning. I wasn't scared … I knew everything would work out the way it should, but just for a split second after the girls were born, I felt empty. I was lying alone (everyone had left the room to take our girls to the neonatal unit), and for the first time ever, I understood how it felt to let go.

My sister, who already had three children, told me I should walk as soon as I could after giving birth. I had to go and see our babies, so I walked across to the neonatal unit that afternoon. I didn't stay long that first visit—I was weak and tired and knew that our babies were in excellent hands. They were so tiny (little skeletons, actually) that I was afraid to touch them. Jade was the smallest at 3.08

pounds, Kaeley weighed 3.21 pounds, and Tayden weighed 3.6 pounds. After that, they lost another 7 ounces or so each, and we had to bring their weight up to 4.4 pounds before we could take them home.

When I returned to my ward, the head nurse brought a double breast pump, and we started to stimulate my breasts for milk every four hours. We didn't get any on the first try, but by the second, we were rewarded with some yellow liquid. They say this is like gold for babies, especially if they are premature like mine were. I couldn't do much for my babies while they were in the ICU, so I focused on providing them with breast milk.

When I was about four months pregnant, I had dreamt that I was giving birth naturally. When the first baby came, I knew she was way too small to survive (since I was only at four months), so I quickly pressed her to my breasts in a crazy attempt to save her. She started to suckle, and soon after that she seemed fine. When the next one started coming, I handed her to my husband and did the same. This went on until they were all born, all fed, and all fine.

When I woke up, I knew that I would need to breastfeed my babies and that it might even save their lives. I often receive guidance through my dreams. There's nothing better than breast milk to help babies become strong and healthy in those first few fragile months. I was amazed at the amount of milk my B-cup breasts were able to produce and also very impressed with God for having created something so amazing. By the time our girls were three months old, I was producing two and a half liters (about ten and a half cups) of milk every 24 hours. To think I had once wished these breasts away!

The babies were in the ICU for six weeks, and we visited them all the time, learning everything we could from the competent and wonderful nurses in the neonatal unit. It was traumatic to leave my girls there, but I was struggling physically and I didn't feel very well at all. I needed to take time to recover, so I was thankful for the help at that stage.

The stretching from the pregnancy had given me anal cramps that caused excruciating pain that I still suffer from today when I ovulate. It was my domestic worker of ten years who advised me to put something strong and elastic around my stretched tummy to tuck it in. (I went out immediately and bought a couple of "Bridget Jones" panties.) My hormones were raging and I felt like crying all the time; actually, I did cry all the time. I especially remember a particular moment at the hospital: I had not yet tried to breastfeed two of the girls at once, and one of the nurses suggested I have a go at it. I struggled, and soon an audience had gathered as everyone tried to help me by pulling here and tugging there … it was all just too much for me and I sobbed! Later, at home with my girls, alone and calm, I managed to feed two of them together all the time. It was such a wonderful, nurturing feeling; I will treasure it forever.

One night I was violently ill, throwing up with nonstop diarrhea. I soon realized that my body was detoxifying. I had been on a lot of medication to prevent me from going into labor too early, and the cortisone injections had also been too much for my system. I had been prepared for babies, but I wasn't prepared for this!

Eventually my doctor recommended a tablet to help with my hormone imbalance and milk production. It worked, but I only took one a day because I'm not fond of using medication. I also dreaded the thought of how my body would react when I stopped taking it. Six months later when I stopped expressing milk for the girls, I stopped taking the tablet and continued to struggle with my hormones. I have heard that it takes a woman's body two years to return to normal after a pregnancy; it took mine three. Three exhausting years. Sometimes my husband and I are still amazed that we survived them.

Becoming a mother was one of the most wonderful blessings I have ever experienced. I have to admit, though, that going through it once was enough for me, so I feel very blessed that all three of my little girls decided to arrive together—and I couldn't be happier about the fact that they are all girls! Today my husband and I put serious strain on our bodies carrying the girls around, and we often beg each other for back massages. I've also put on a few pounds from simply not having enough time to look after myself, but I know what I have to do to get in shape again. I'll start by loving myself enough and making time for myself.

BODY BONDING

Our bodies need three things to assist us properly on our journey: nourishment, exercise, and unconditional love. If we can love and accept our bodies unconditionally, give them the nutrition they need, and stay active, they will be able to help us enjoy our lives to the fullest. Someone once referred to the body as "our vehicle here on Earth." Just as our vehicles need fuel and regular services to remain reliable, so do our bodies.

If we can love and accept our bodies unconditionally … they will be able to help us enjoy our lives to the fullest.

Here are a few of the things I do to take care of my body lovingly. Please bear in mind that we are all unique and what works for me might not necessarily work for you. I just hope that this will inspire you to find out what does.

I LISTEN TO MY BODY

Louise Hay is one of my favorite authors, and I often refer to her book *Heal Your Body*[1] to understand what my body is trying to say to me. Our thoughts and feelings have a physical effect on our bodies, and it's very useful to be able to understand these connections. The healing process is also much more powerful when we confront the emotional cause of a problem, rather than only focusing on its physical aspect. This approach empowers us by allowing us to take responsibility for our health, or lack of it.

I CHOOSE TO BE FABULOUS

I am fabulous! And when I forget it, I stand in front of my mirror and tell myself that I am fabulous over and over again. I look for something I like about myself, and I focus on that until I feel fabulous.

Being and feeling fabulous are choices, and I choose to be fabulous.

If I still don't feel fabulous, I do whatever it takes to make me feel fabulous. If it's going to make me feel fabulous to eat healthfully, I do that … or exercise or dress up and go out and have some fun … being fabulous and feeling fabulous are choices, and I choose to be fabulous.

I GIVE MY BODY WHAT IT NEEDS

Dietitian Maryke Bronkhorst has the following to say:

> Minor changes in your eating habits can lead to major changes in your health. What you eat not only affects your day-to-day health, but also helps to determine the quality of your life and even how long you will live.
>
> Nutrition is still a young science, but it is clear that there are few ailments that diet cannot help to prevent, cure, or at least make more bearable. Nutrient intake out of balance with nutrient needs is linked to many leading

causes of morbidity and mortality, including obesity, heart disease, cancer, liver disease, and diabetes.

That is why a healthy diet is of utmost importance, a diet that will prevent or minimize your risk of developing nutrition-related diseases and make you healthy from within.[2]

With Maryke's guidance, I have been able to recognize what my body needs and figure out what works for me:

- **I drink my vegetables and eat my fruit:** I have juice made from celery (±3.5 fluid ounces), spinach (±3.5 fluid ounces), and carrot (±17 fluid ounces) three times a day and try to eat at least three fruits every day. My girls also drink vegetable juices three times a day … I add apples to sweeten theirs.
- **I drink lots of water:** I enjoy a cup of coffee or rooibos tea accompanied by a Ferrero Rocher every day, and I enjoy a glass of merlot every now and then, but other than that, I drink water. I was shocked when my dietitian told me how much sugar there is in carbonated drinks, and I gave them up completely. Today, I don't even miss them.
- **More protein, less starch:** If I want to lose a few pounds, or just maintain my weight, I focus on increasing my protein intake and keeping my starch intake low. My body has difficulty digesting protein and starch together, so I try not to mix the two. I also prefer not to eat starch at suppertime, so if I do include it, I'll have it with lunch, but in general I try to avoid it because my body reacts negatively to it. If I eat starch, I crave more starch and I can't seem to get satisfied … I just keep feeling hungry. Starch also affects my mood; I often feel grumpy and depressed if I eat too much of it. When it comes to protein, I focus on white meats like chicken and fish. My favorite fish is salmon, which I prefer to eat raw with some ginger, soy sauce, and wasabi. There are a lot more nutrients in raw food than in cooked food.
- **Eat less, more often:** I eat small portions frequently to speed up my metabolism. Often, when we want to lose weight, we stop eating, and this is a mistake; it slows our metabolism and makes our bodies think we are starving, so they store whatever we eat, making it harder to lose weight. Sumo wrestlers gain weight by eating one huge meal a day at suppertime—so if you want to gain weight, this is the way to do it.

EXERCISE

I used to do high-cardio workouts without any positive results. I would sweat up a storm, just to end up aching everywhere and feeling hungry all the time. This made it very challenging for me to maintain my goal weight. Exercise is very important, but maintaining your goal weight depends mostly on what you eat. My current personal trainer, Nicolette Lodge, is a great inspiration to me, and the change and improvement in my body has been amazing. We are all unique, so we need to listen to our bodies; they will tell us whether or not our training methods are working for us.

Nicolette is a core-strength trainer who has developed her style from many different disciplines. She is basically self-taught, and prefers to find her own way of solving the mysteries that each individual client presents. She has an out-of-the-box approach to teaching and a passion for empowering clients to become their own teachers and healers. I asked Nicolette to try to condense her exercise routine into a few words, and she was kind enough to share the following:

Here's the long and short of it: If a person's heart is good, the person is good. If the core of an apple is rotten, the apple is rotten. If a building's foundations are shaky, the building is condemned.

I always begin my client's training program by focusing on his or her core. This is of utmost importance, as can be seen in the above examples. If you try to pile weight onto a shaky foundation, the structure will collapse.

So where is this elusive core that everyone talks about? Draw a line across the center of your body dividing top and bottom, and another dividing your right and left sides, and voilà! You have located the core. Your core muscles are your stabilizers, the ones that hold you upright, give you good posture, and give strength to your skeleton. Remember: Without muscles, we would literally collapse in a heap on the floor. It is our muscles that hold us upright—not our skeletons, as most people think.

I scan my client, looking for imbalances. I check the shoulder height and the spine, hip, knee, ankle, and foot alignment for symmetry. If one muscle group is tight (for instance, the right shoulder), I scan down the body and will invariably find that the opposite hip is out of alignment, which may then reflect in the opposite knee or ankle. I monitor the distribution of weight in the body. Are the shoulders centered over the hips? And are those centered evenly between the feet?

I start my client by limbering up all the external muscles with arm swinging, breathing, rolling up and down through the spine, circling the hips and shoulders, bending sideways, and twisting the spine gently, never forcibly.

Then I measure the degree of muscle imbalance in the pelvis and hips, and the length of the legs. If there is a difference, I will use techniques such as Muscle Activation and acupressure or a combination of techniques to encourage the relaxation of tight muscles and restore neutral alignment.

When the body is straight and symmetrical, we perform Muscle Activation to various pressure points on the body. This enables the muscles to perform to their full capacity.

When all the muscles are activated and the posture correct, we begin with abdominal work. We use breathing as a focus to ensure the client does not strain, and capitalize on the correct contraction and relaxation of the muscles involved.

I teach my clients how to "zip up" and engage their layers from the innermost core. We use a lot of visualization techniques that are often done with eyes closed, as opposed to staring at the outer muscles in the mirror at the gym.

Once my client is able to engage the abdominal muscles with ease, we focus on the back muscles. I always balance my training by alternating work on the muscles on the front of the body with the corresponding muscles at the back (e.g., abs then back, right side followed by left side, quadriceps followed by hamstrings).

After each muscle group has been worked, we stretch the muscles for upwards of 30 seconds until complete relaxation has been achieved. Stretching is a vital part of my training program, as it promotes greater flexibility, recovery, and strength.

If my client has a particular weakness in one muscle group, we will spend more time on that area to strengthen it. For example, if the right thigh is weaker than the left, we may do 20 reps on the right leg and only 10 on the left, or we may just train the weaker leg.

I have incorporated many different disciplines in my work. These include my earliest ballet training, aerobic and gym training, physiotherapy and occupational therapy exercises, yoga, Muscle Activation, acupressure techniques, meditation, and breathing techniques. I have gathered these various styles along my journey and tested them all before introducing them to my clients. My training involves problem solving and trial and error. Each client's program is individually tailored to his or her specific needs, strengths, and weaknesses.

I generally don't ask my clients to do a lot of repetitions, but ask them to focus on correct alignment when executing movements. It is quite amazing how much more effective a few well-executed exercises can be compared to fast repetitions, which rely on momentum rather than muscle strength.[3]

HELPING MYSELF TO SUCCEED

Knowing myself helps a lot. I usually start craving unhealthy snacks either when I am very tired or when I am watching television, and if there is an unhealthy snack in the house at that point, I know I won't be able to resist it. I often feel like one of Pavlov's dogs … when my television set is turned on, I immediately start feeling hungry—even if I have just had a big meal! They call this "classical conditioning" in psychology. I also know that I simply cannot resist potato chips and fatty, wet biltong (beef jerky)—so if I want to eat healthfully, I simply don't buy them.

If we understand the reasons for our behavior, it becomes easier to eliminate unhealthy habits.

In addition to keeping unhealthy food out of my house, I have realized that if I understand the reasons for my behavior, it becomes easier to eliminate unhealthy habits. If my mind is occupied while watching television, I don't think about food, so now I often work on my laptop when the TV goes on. Adequate rest and keeping busy also help tremendously to control those cravings.

CHOOSING ALTERNATIVE OPTIONS

Although I know and understand that mainstream medicine has a very important place in the world today, I prefer to check all my options before taking any medication. I believe that we have become too impatient … always wanting a quick fix.

The problem is that these quick fixes often only last a little while and almost always have side effects. They only numb the pain, and because the emotional root of the problem has not been healed, the illness often returns. I have been on a few antidepressants; they were a nice crutch for a while, but eventually I needed to walk on my own again. I never felt quite myself while I was taking them—I enjoy being in control of my emotions and my life, and this was almost like being on autopilot. There are so many effective alternative options; I would like to share a few that have worked for me. Once again, keep in mind that we are all different and unique, so only you can decide what works for you.

SCIO

The SCIO is a sophisticated biofeedback system designed for stress detection and stress reduction. It does *not* diagnose any clinical diseases. The SCIO measures the unconscious of the patient, and provides an interface between the conscious and unconscious minds. The unconscious monitors the total complexity of life experience. Since the conscious mind is only aware of a tiny fraction of the totality of exposure, it is not a reliable source of information for life or disease. The device gathers bio-energetic data from the body via 55 parameters simultaneously. This happens at biological speed, which is one-hundredth of a second for each stimulus. This means that thousands of items can be screened for reactions from the body in a few minutes. Imbalances at the energetic or subtle-energy level can be early warning signs regarding health status. If imbalances go uncorrected, eventually physical symptoms will erupt, and health problems and disease develop. In addition to being an early prophylactic, keeping subtle energies balanced helps restore physical energy.

The SCIO communicates with the body to determine which energy imbalances are affecting personal health most: physical, mental, or emotional concerns. It is calibrated to measure the body's subtle reactions to a database of biological, psychological, and medical items in electromagnetic form. The sensitivity is set so finely that it picks up the earliest sign of disease and distress. The information is then prioritized to help the practitioner zero in on the body's current specific needs. The program offers information specific to subtle energies—emotional and mental stresses, nutritional needs, toxins, food sensitivities, digestive and elimination needs, etc. The values shown represent an 85 percent probability that the body has reacted to that particular signal.

Evaluation and treatment: For best results, a highly trained practitioner needs to evaluate these readings. By analyzing recurring patterns, he or she will be able to give information about issues that may be below conscious recognition, such as mental and emotional stresses, nutritional suggestions, food sensitivities, and digestive and elimination needs. The energetic imbalances are identified by the SCIO in order of the body's priorities. Treatment is thus similar to peeling an onion; each session will work with the outermost layer. The SCIO applies the appropriate frequencies to help correct the imbalances and allow the body to shift gear into a state of greater health and vitality. The subconscious indicates which treatments or remedies are most appropriate for each individual. The practitioner will recommend nutritional supplements and lifestyle changes based on their ability to boost the body's energy fields. The practitioner will apply his or her clinical judgement to determine the core illness, frequency of treatments needed, and strategy for subsequent sessions. In order to get the most out of a SCIO session, the patient needs to accept responsibility for his or her health and be prepared to implement the recommended lifestyle changes.[4]

Metamorphosis

The philosophy of Metamorphosis is open to anyone interested in the idea of fundamental self-healing. Conceived by Robert St. John in the late 1930s, its aim is to create balance and stability. It brings freedom from negative unconscious memories and genetic influences from the past. The negative memories are "blocks" that are registered at conception and determine the attitude of mind toward life. All illness and disease, whether it be mental, physical, emotional, or behavioral, stems from the primary attitudes of mind introduced at conception and developed during gestation. Metamorphosis eliminates these negative attitudes, allowing us to live creatively in the present moment. Living "in the moment" releases anxiety and the future becomes a creation. Being a creator means that one can live life in a harmonious and stress-free way. Metamorphosis addresses the disturbance or source of the block in treatment. As we transform our blocks, the memories of symptoms are forgotten. The healing is fundamental and therefore permanent. Metamorphosis is not a scientific approach, but it is interesting to note that scientists are now aware that our DNA holds memory of life going back millions of years. Two scientists, James Watson and Francis Crick, discovered cell memory back in the 1950s.[5]

Chiropractic

This is a system of treating disease by manipulation of the vertebral column. Chiropractic is based on the theory that most diseases are caused by pressure on the nerves because of faulty alignment of the bones, especially the vertebrae, and that the nerves are thus prevented from transmitting to various organs of the body the neural impulses for proper functioning.[6]

Louise Hay

Recently dubbed "the closest thing to a living saint" by the Australian media, the octogenarian Louise Hay is also known as one of the founders of the self-help movement. Through Louise's healing techniques and positive philosophy, millions have learned how to create more of what they want in their lives, including more wellness in their bodies, minds, and spirits. Louise was able to put her philosophies into practice when she was diagnosed with cancer. She considered alternatives to surgery and drugs, and instead developed an intensive program of affirmations, visualization, nutritional cleansing, and psychotherapy. Within six months she was completely healed.[7]

Brain Gym®

Brain Gym rewires the brain through movement. It "switches the brain on" for any goal of our choice, making it easier to achieve. In addition to the mind, the physical body also needs to be ready in order to support us in pursuit of our goals. For example, if our goal is to increase our income, we literally will not be able to see the opportunities that come our way if our eyes are not "switched on."

NAET

NAET stands for Numbudripad's Allergy Elimination Technique. This is a drug-free solution for allergies, including hay fever, eczema, and gluten intolerance. Depression, ADD/ADHD, and many other diseases have a strong allergy component. Very good results have been seen in healing these diseases. The combination of Brain Gym and NAET is very powerful. NAET is also very effective in learning to let go of limiting and negative beliefs.[8]

MY MIND

Men and women are not prisoners of fate,
but only prisoners of their own minds.

— FRANKLIN D. ROOSEVELT

Our minds are fascinating. It has been extremely liberating for me to discover how my mind works, and also very comforting to realize that "I" am not my mind. I love the fact that I can control my mind and improve the way it functions. There are no limits, except for those that I place there myself.

I used to think of myself as very average in the "brains department." I struggled in school and only achieved average grades even though I studied diligently. I was advised to drop math early in high school—which is interesting, because people with musical talent are usually also good at math, since both use the same parts of the brain. However, it used to take me about three pages to work out a two-line sum, and then I would still get the answer wrong. I graduated in the top portion of my class, but all my subjects were memory work.

By the time I left school, my general knowledge wasn't very good, and I often found myself in embarrassing situations because of that. I have always been interested in only two things in life: people and music. I am fascinated by human behavior and very sensitive to people's emotions and energies, and I pick up on pain and sadness immediately. This is one of the reasons why I am prone to depression; my empathy for others can often make me feel very sad, and I constantly have to remind myself not to confuse other people's feelings with my own. Before I became aware of this, I felt as though I lived in a tumble dryer of ups and downs, but thankfully I've learned how to tell these feelings apart now. It has also been very liberating to be in control of my emotions. It's made my life so much easier.

When I started my own business, I realized that I was actually not all that useless at math. I managed to balance my own books for a while, and I also figured out how to use Word and Excel on a computer without any help. Many years prior to starting my company, I had an analysis done that revealed that I used the right side of my brain (the creative side) predominantly. A few years later, a second analysis showed that both sides of my brain were now more equally engaged (although the right brain was still dominant). Being forced to do my own admin work, managing my bookings, and making all the necessary arrangements has helped me develop the left side of my brain.

I have done numerous tests over the years in an effort to understand my mind and the impact it has had on my life more clearly, and getting to know myself has played an incredibly important role in helping me improve my quality of life. Before we realize that we are in control of our minds and emotions, we can easily be swept away by irrational behavior, depression, and the constant struggle to maintain healthy relationships. A wise electrician once said to me, "You can't stop a bird from flying over your head, but you can stop it from building a nest there."

You can't stop a bird from flying over your head, but you can stop it from building a nest there.

Earlier, I wrote about lacking the confidence to speak to people and feeling uncomfortable around people. Here are the results of a personality test I did recently. I am sharing this to show that it is possible to grow in areas that don't come naturally to us. The test was the Myers-Briggs Type Indicator, according to which there are 16 personality types. Mine turned out to be the ENFJ (Extrovert/Intuiting/Feeling/Judging):

ENFJs are defined as warm and outgoing, including others in their conversations and activities and facilitating interaction. They are perceptive about people, and their great strength lies in seeing and supporting the positive potential in others. Change is exciting to ENFJs. They readily look for and find possibilities in new situations. Their understanding of others and their enthusiasm can make them inspiring leaders and catalysts. They are fiercely loyal to those whose values and commitment they respect. Change can also present difficulties for ENFJs; however, their focus on people means that they take anyone's negative feelings about change seriously. They have a hard time dealing with conflict and real differences between people. Their primary commitment is to people, not institutions; they can become very upset if their values are not considered and supported.[9]

As you can see, I still have to work on dealing with conflict and learn how to handle it when my values are not supported.

I have also taken the Thomas-Kilmann Conflict Mode Instrument (TKI) Test[10] and worked my way through the different conflict modes, which are competing, col-

laborating, compromising, avoiding, and accom-
modating. I found the suggestions and information
very helpful, and know that I will be able to improve
the way I deal with conflict by applying them.

Another test I took not so long ago was an
emotional intelligence test, and after the results
were explained to me, I felt so inspired that I immediately wrote the song "I Walk with You." The
test confirmed what I already knew, but somehow it just made things fall into place for me
and helped me embrace that part of myself so much more.

Once we understand ourselves, we can really start to grow and develop our minds and our personalities, and learn how to be in control of our emotions.

Once we understand ourselves, we can really start to grow, develop our minds
and our personalities, and learn how to be in control of our emotions. But we first
need to be honest with ourselves and take responsibility.

Doing self-help tests is one way of getting to know more about ourselves, but
the people close to us can also help us. If you want to see whether or not you have
grown as a person, ask a few friends and family members to write down the changes
they have seen in you (if any) so that you can take stock and see if there has been any
growth. This will also help you identify areas where you still need to grow.

I decided to do this myself, and here is what my husband, my parents, and two
of my dearest friends wrote about me:

What my husband, Andrew Thompson, who has known me for 14 years now, said:

When I collected Sonia at her apartment for our very first date, she had
flooded her flat and wasn't really doing anything to stop the water damage
(actually, she was just sitting on the bed, watching the water flow down the
stairs). I knew then that I had a serious challenge on my hands—but since
then, Sonia has really grown. From being a dilly [absentminded] musician,
she has learned to adapt to her environment and become more business-
minded, computer literate, and fluent in English after coming from a very
Afrikaans background.

As usual, I can't resist the urge to elaborate on what my husband said. I remember
that day; I was overwhelmed by that watery mess and numbed by the prospect of

cleaning it. Thankfully, Andrew loves cleaning up a mess, so we really are a perfect couple! Even though I haven't changed much when it comes to cleaning, at least I haven't flooded the house in about nine years now, so I've definitely grown in that area! It's wonderful to be in "la la land," and I've spent most of my life there, but the fact remains that I am here in the real world, and if I want to cope, I need to be aware of the world and the people around me. I need to focus and pay attention; when I do, my life becomes more manageable. It also becomes easier for others to be with me.

I think that writing a book in English (which is my second language) is also quite an accomplishment, and my husband would agree. In the beginning he spent a lot of time correcting my grammar and explaining words to me.

What my father said:

I would say that you were more of an introvert as a toddler, although laughter came easily to you. Most of the time, you had a shy little laugh, but you could go into absolute spasms if you thought something was really funny. You had a strong will that you exercised instinctively, and when I teased you, you would get so upset that tears would well up in your eyes. I was always fascinated by your strong sense of justice—and you expressed your own opinions, even when you were very little. You would also become very excited about new projects and take a leading role.

When you became a teenager, you withdrew more and more into your music. You insisted on having your way, and I often told you that you thought you were the queen of the house. Later I realized that crossing swords with you was counterproductive. There was a lot of conflict between us until the day you said, "Dad, when did you last give me a hug and tell me that you love me?" I admired your courage and prayed for you often.

Many of your qualities emerged when you became a mother. I have experienced your increasing understanding of love—what it means to support and encourage others. You are a shining example of generosity, and you live the truth, "It is better to give than to receive." I am extremely proud of the way you have grown from a relatively self-absorbed teenager into an inspiring woman.

What my mother said:

You were the sweetest little baby. We didn't get a wink of sleep the first few nights we had you at home, and then we realized that we were bothering you; you wanted to sleep in a room of your own. You were always a solitary child; all through primary school and high school, you only ever had one friend, and you didn't visit each other very often and never slept over.

When you were very little, you often went off on excursions of your own to explore the world, and Jasper, our Scottish terrier, would follow you faithfully. Once, a man found you in the street about four blocks away from home. He stopped you, took your hand, and followed Jasper back to the house. Naturally it was very traumatic for me to think that I hadn't even known where you were. But you were still "Missy Perfect"—"Look Mommy, I'm not being naughty, and I'm clean."

You did your schoolwork meticulously and spent hours with your books … you also spent hours fantasizing about your dreams, but you never got into trouble regarding your schoolwork. You would definitely have flourished in a school [with an arts focus] like Pro Arte, but the money simply wasn't there.

You hated practicing your piano pieces, but spent hours playing your own songs. You would listen to your pieces once, and after that, you wanted to play them in your own way; you never saw any point in practicing them over and over again. Naturally, this was a terrible disappointment to your music teachers who didn't appreciate your creativity and incredible talent. One teacher stated that you wouldn't go very far in the music world, but it was just like you to develop the determination to believe in what you knew you wanted to—and could—achieve. In high school, there were two music teachers who did discover your soul and encourage you to follow your dream—a dream that has been realized in the celebrated work you've done so far. At least you received a bursary [scholarship] so that you could study music.

You would often lock horns with your father when you felt he was too critical of me. You would try to protect me, and he would tell you that you thought you were the queen of the house to put you in your place.

I guess you were the odd one out at high school; no extreme fashion trends for you. You loved beautiful dresses and sandals, and you would plan what you were going to wear to an occasion for hours. Once, on a school tour, you persisted with your style while everyone else went dressed comfortably in sneakers and shorts. I also teased you often, but you were happy with yourself; as far as you were concerned, the problem lay with everyone else, and you never doubted yourself. Another thing about you … you never hit back; you just turned the other cheek. Sometimes I felt sorry that I never taught you to fight back, but I wasn't like that, either, and you were probably following my example. Both of us just wanted peace and quiet.

You shared everything with me. From your first love bite to your wild student days, you always asked for and accepted my advice. We are, and were, unbelievably close to each other, more than what I was to the other children, not because I loved them less, but because you opened up to me and held nothing back.

The book *Conversations With God*[11] changed your whole life. You started sparkling—you still followed your dream, heart and soul, but now you had a different point of view. The caring Nianell came out of the closet and started motivating people and proclaiming love.

I was convinced that if you ever fell pregnant, you would only do it once, so I prayed for a miracle and *voilà*—triplets.

There is also a Sonia who wants to do things now, immediately—then you say things like, "Please don't disturb me, I'm watching this DVD" or, "I don't want to be around people right now—I'm staying in my room," but we all have to look after ourselves like that sometimes.

Your determination to carry on believing in yourself has borne fruit. Your belief in the higher power, in being ethical, in sharing, and above all proving love to your fellow man has made you an example. Life's Gift.

What a dear male friend said:
Wow … my friend Sonia has asked me to write a little about her growth as a person. She asked me this afternoon and she needs it tomorrow! That in itself says a lot about her and her crazy life. I met Nia in 1990 at what was then called the Pretoria Technikon. We were both first-year students, both very green, and both convinced that the world deserved to hear our talent. My first impression of Nia was that of a little buck caught in the headlights of an oncoming car. She was shy, conscious of her faults, emotional, and very sad to be so far from home. I seem to remember that she cried a lot. I also remember thinking she was hot! She had wild curly hair and a raw beauty that

didn't need makeup to highlight it. I was by far the biggest nerd in the class (I thought I was the coolest dude, though) … I wore glasses the size of plates, I was very chubby, and I think she became my friend because she took pity on me. Those initial impressions have developed into a beautiful friendship that has lasted for more than 20 years and will undoubtedly continue for the rest of our lives. I also remember that she used to ask a lot of (what I thought were) the silliest questions. I remember thinking, "Can this girl be this naive? Is she really this dumb?" I had never, up till that point, met the proverbial dumb blonde. She was it—with dark hair. Much later, I realized that she was teaching me a *very* important life lesson: If you don't ask, you don't get. That goes for everything, from knowledge to business to love and to life as a whole. As I got to know her, I soon realized she had some serious talent.

We have worked together in a few bands, some formed by us and some by friends, continuously hiring and firing each other, and we have played in the country's worst pubs. I still remember one particularly drunk patron at a nowhere pub asking me if I could ask her to shut up and sing myself in-stead—he couldn't take her operatic twist on Tina Turner's "Simply the Best"!

I saw something else in her those first years—an unwavering determina-tion and belief in herself. Am I surprised at her success today? Not one bit. Her talent hasn't changed. Her execution of it has just improved. She has changed, though. If anyone were to ask me what my overall feeling is when I think of what Sonia has become, that feeling would be pride. I am so very proud of her. Not in the way that most people who know her casually are (for her voice or incredible songwriting ability)—I am proud of her growth as a person and as a soul. She has learned so very much. From someone whom I initially thought was pretty scatterbrained, she has become a mas-ter of business in the music industry. She also sucks the very marrow out of life and really just gets what this ride is all about. That's what I am so proud of. Does she still have her faults? Of course she does. Don't we all?

She still doesn't listen—I mean really listen—sometimes when she should. She's trying, though. She's a bad friend in the traditional sense of the word—if you want someone to remember your birthday, pop around for tea, or shoot the breeze about the latest movie, she is not your girl. I prefer what she does do, though: defend her family and her friends to the death. She also has a built-in empathy and an intuitive ability to say just what needs to be said to make things right. After my wife, she would be my first call if I really needed serious help. And even if she was in New York or on the moon, I would trust her to get to me. That's what you rely upon and trust in a true friend.

What a dear female friend said:

I met Sonia (Nianell), my soul friend, 7 years ago … or is it 7,000 years? A friendship with her cannot be defined in time. She wears her heart on her sleeve … before you can even wonder what she is feeling, she'll tell you. About five minutes after we met, her first question—one of many to me—was, "Don't you feel very lonely without a husband?" I remember bursting out laughing … she was so naively honest and always had the ability to make me laugh. I remember the silliest moments: when we were very late picking up the band, and doing some "low-flying" over too-many-to-count speed bumps on the way to the airport. I can still hear her saying, "Oh my … and now I must still try to look like Nianell." I must be honest—at that stage I couldn't understand how anyone could take so long to make themselves up at all … but this came to a sudden end with the birth of her triplet girls, who definitely succeeded in minimizing her time in front of the mirror!

After a show, her energy levels could take her right through the night and anyone who dared even to look sleepy would be given a soft but firm smack to bring them back to the conversation. Her responsibility as a parent now drives her back home after a show so that she can be with the girls in the morning.

It astonishes me how determined Sonia can be when she puts her mind to something … I saw her shrinking by about 30 pounds after she had put her mind to following a healthy lifestyle … and she keeps it up amid all sorts of temptations from everyone, everywhere, all wanting to spoil her.

In those early days of our friendship, Sonia could easily have been studying for a master's degree in self-analysis. Nowadays she might just pass …

I always said that she must have been born with the ability to see the world in 3D … the small, less important details remain somewhere in the distance while the things that really matter are dominant and excitingly visible in what she says and the way she lives life. Anyone who's ever tried to talk to her about handbags, hats, or high heels will agree with that.

Her desire to motivate and inspire people around the globe has seemed even stronger than her ambition to be a successful singer/songwriter at times … and this was where I met her … her career, well on the go … but her heart and mind filled with questions about how to achieve this. At that time she still hovered between three very dominant personalities: the darling, dear Sonia with the magic in her eyes, the Nia who needed confirmation that she was heading in the right direction, and the immaculate artist Nianell. Her special relationship with time has always intrigued me … and somehow as time has gone by, she has managed to turn these three personalities into a single, very balanced whole.

What a privilege it has been to see her soaring into the world of wisdom, and to witness how this perspective has turned those questions from way back into answers. It's really a challenge to try to sum up someone with such a big heart in a few lines; but I don't know anyone else in whose company I feel closer to our Creator.

Looking back and remembering some of the mistakes I made, I cringe at the thought that I might have hurt people, and it's a little hard to accept some of the things I did when I was inexperienced and ignorant … but then I tell myself, "Sometimes we have to be who we are not, to find out who we are."

Sometimes we have to be who we are not, to find out who we are.

What we focus on will grow, so I choose to focus on how I can improve myself and my life.

DEPRESSION

"What's the use? What's the point of it all?"

These were questions that I often struggled with. Why do some people suffer from depression while others seem to cope—or do they? Do some of us experience life more intensely? Why is that?

Emotional vacillations can be really tiring, but they also have their benefits … if I always felt great, I would have nothing to compare that with and would not appreciate the "ups" as much as I do.

The "downs" can be really exhausting. To me, it felt like I was trapped on a little boat on the big ocean in the middle of a serious storm with no help—just me, and the storm raging inside and around me. My first serious depression was the most distressing one because I had not yet learned any survival skills, so there was nothing to hold on to while the storm passed. I just wanted to sleep all the time. Sometimes I would hide away under the dashboard of my car in a deserted parking lot. I couldn't even speak to my mother, with whom I usually share everything. I felt loveless, and that scared me into numbness. I experienced panic attacks. First, my right arm and the right side of my face would go numb, and then the numbness would lead to something worse—a locked jaw. This was very uncomfortable and inconvenient; I am a singer and pianist, after all—I need my jaw and arms in working condition … imagine trying to play the piano with a numb arm or trying to sing with spit running from the side of your mouth.

We need to understand our reasons for depression if we want to gain control of it. There are many things that can bring us down: feeling lonely or rejected, being overworked, having nothing to do, financial problems, health problems, guilt, fear, feeling helpless or worthless—the list is endless.

I've narrowed my depression down to the following: If I haven't had enough rest and "me time," I end up feeling down; my hormones can bring me down at a certain time of the month; and I've also discovered that I am a bit of an adrenaline junkie—the thrill of a performance puts me on a "high" that lasts for about two days and then I fall.

Before I understood the reasons for it, depression really confused and scared me. This made me feel helpless, and then things would spin out of control very quickly. I would find fault with everything and everyone—but mostly with myself—and everything in my life would feel wrong. If I had remained in control and retained a grip on reality, this overwhelming problem could have remained a minor issue.

We need to know and understand our minds in the same way we do our bodies. If we don't, they can take control and leave us feeling helpless.

This is what Louise L. Hay writes about depression:

Problem: Depression
Probable cause: Anger you feel you do not have a right to have. Hopelessness.
New thought pattern: I now go beyond other people's fears and limitations. I create my life.[12]

I am proud to report that I haven't experienced a panic attack for many years now. You see, I have realized that depression is like a circle that becomes smaller and smaller all the time. The first circle is very big and to get around it takes ages,

We need to know and understand our minds.

but as it becomes smaller, things normalize more quickly. Also, I know I've made it through the storm once, so I know I can do it again—it's just a matter of time before I will feel better.

There are a number of things that I do to help myself stay afloat during this "sitting and waiting it out" time. I call them "mind maintenance."

MIND MAINTENANCE

- **Positive affirmation:** I start by repeating a "new thought pattern" by Louise Hay to myself daily: I CREATE MY LIFE! I CREATE MY LIFE! I CREATE MY LIFE! I CREATE MY LIFE! I CREATE MY LIFE! Just saying this line makes me feel great!

- **Eat healthfully:** I eat nutritious foods and try not to eat myself to death, which is what I usually want to do when I feel low! I stay away from carbohydrates—they make me feel even more depressed, and once I've had carbohydrates, I'll crave more of them. Before I know it, I will have another reason to feel depressed!

- **Keep your mind off yourself:** I try not to hide away from the world. This is not a good time to spend a lot of time with myself because I am not good company right now. I spend time with happy, uplifting, positive people. If that makes me feel even more depressed, I try helping someone who feels even worse than I do. In other words, I do whatever I can to keep my mind off myself! I find helping others extremely uplifting and healing, as I do spending time with uplifting, positive people.

- **Be creative:** Being creative is also great medicine for depression. Write down your feelings, paint a picture, write a song, plant some seeds in your garden, dance—whatever form of creativity works for you.

- **Walk it off:** I get my happy juices (endorphins) flowing by exercising. I love walking—especially in nature. If you are physically limited, remember how powerful your mind is. Imagine yourself exercising and visualize it into effectiveness! Dr. Vinoth Ranganathan and his team at the Cleveland Clinic performed an experiment in which a team of 30 young adults were asked to imagine contracting either the muscle of their little fingers or their elbow flexors as vividly as they were able to. They did this for five minutes daily, five days a week for 12 weeks. When compared to a control group, they had increased their pinkie muscle strength by 35 percent and their elbow strength by 13.4 percent. Brain scans taken after the study also showed greater and more focused activity in the prefrontal cortex than before. The researchers determined that their strength gains were due to improvements in the brain's ability to signal muscle. So just by imagining exercise, you can get your happy juices flowing.

- **Brain Gym®:** For me, this remains the best way to eliminate negative and unsupportive thoughts and reprogram my mind.
- **Pretend:** Pretend that you are a celebrity being interviewed for a popular magazine. I remember answering questions for an interview once, and while answering them, I started to feel so much better. Why don't you try it? While you answer the questions, pretend that everyone knows who you are and that your answers might go out there and influence someone's life.

Below is the interview from a few years ago that lifted my spirit and inspired me to be more loving toward myself and take control. Adapt the questions to what is relevant for you in your life. These were my answers at the time:

My favorite things:
1. Healthy snack: *I eat a lot of apples*
2. Destination: *Yzerfontein, West Coast; and Swakopmund, Namibia*
3. Season: *Autumn*
4. Movie: *The Green Mile*
5. Fruit: *Apple*
6. Vegetable: *Gem squash*
7. Quote: *If you spot it, you've got it*

Stats:
1. Occupation: *Singer/songwriter*
2. Age: *38*

3. Family members: *I have two sisters, my parents, a husband, and triplets*

4. Residence: *Cape Town and Johannesburg*

5. How did your musical career start? Would you like your children to follow in your footsteps? *My mom says I was born on a note. I wrote songs from a very early age and always knew that music was my life. After school I studied music and then went straight into the music industry. My girls must find what they love, and do what they want to do. I will support and encourage them all the way.*

6. How do you keep yourself and your family healthy while still juggling a successful career? Do you have any tips for working mothers? *I train with a personal trainer and believe that being active is very important. We believe in the 80/20 concept: Eat and live healthfully 80 percent of the time, and then you can go crazy for the other 20 percent. We drink our vegetables (carrot, spinach, celery, and beetroot), and we eat our fruit. We try not to eat too much red meat or mix our starches and proteins. We also take our vitamins, and I believe in Septogard during winter. Oh yes … and drink a lot of water. I love a cup of coffee after lunch, but other than that I only drink water and rooibos tea. We try to stay away from dairy products and bread.*

7. What has been your biggest challenge since the birth of your triplets? With your career involving frequent travel and occasional stress, how do you nurture family closeness? *The biggest challenge has been taking care of myself, because I give all my attention and energy to my children, my husband, and my career, and then there's none left over for me—which has taken its toll. I've just realized again how important it is to take care of yourself, because if you go down, you can't give anything of yourself to others. Exercise and healthy eating is not enough; it's just as important to take time off regularly and REST! That is a challenge for me because I have so many responsibilities.*

8. What does an average day in the life of Nianell look like (a detailed description)? *At around seven-thirty, I train with my trainer while my girls sit with me. We train for one or two hours, but it's also time spent playing with and hugging the girls. After that I spend some more time with them, playing outside for an hour (that's if I don't have interviews or meetings), and then I put them to bed for their afternoon nap. While they sleep, I do my e-mails, which is a full-time job in itself! In the afternoon, we usually have to prepare for a show. If the venue is close by, we will leave in the afternoon—otherwise*

we'll leave in the morning. When we arrive at the venue, we set up, do a sound check, and then I have to turn myself into Miss World for the show. After the show, I like to spend some time with my supporters and stay to talk to them for an hour or two. Then when the gear has been packed, we drive back home. We usually get to bed between midnight and two after shows … and then we start all over again!

9. Where do you find the inspiration to be a good mother and wife? And to be a good performer and singer/songwriter? *God, my husband, my children, my parents, family, friends, people, and nature and everything in it! Life inspires me!*

Life is gold, nothing else is needed.

– Deepak Chopra

10. What is the most valuable health advice you've ever received, and from whom? *To love myself, given by Hanna Kok, my life coach.*[13]

11. Where do you find the energy to be a mom to three kids, a wife, and singer/songwriter, and always keep smiling? *I do what I love and what I am passionate about. I also love my family and I am passionate about their well-being, so I choose always to give them my best. It's not always easy, but at the end of the day, it's a choice—after that, one must just have faith. There are two ways to go through life: smiling or not smiling. I choose to smile!*

12. How do you make time for yourself? And what do you do during this "me time"? *Now there is something I must work on—I find making time for myself very challenging. When the kids go to bed on nights when I don't have a show, I usually just fall into bed and watch a DVD. I love movies—I lose myself in them. I also love to read, and to write in my diary.*

13. What is the most important thing you want to teach your children? And what lasting memory would you like to leave them with? *My children will most probably follow my example, no matter what I try to teach them, so I do my best to love myself at all times because that is the most important love of all. If you love yourself, that means you love God, because He created you. You can only love and respect life and other people once you have learned to love yourself. I would like them to remember how much I loved them, my husband,*

myself, everyone else, nature, animals, life, and God. Keep life uncomplicated, don't allow fear to control you, and just be alive!

14. What have the most amazing moments in your life been so far? *Giving birth to our girls and renewing my wedding vows with my husband on our tenth anniversary; every moment I manage to spend with my husband and our three little angels is amazing.*

15. What does the near future hold? Any exciting projects on the horizon? *I am releasing my second DVD,* Sand & Water, *this year. I have had a few breakthroughs on the international front: I have been nominated for Song of the Year by the L.A. Music Awards and have also been chosen to sing a duet with Andrea Bocelli on July 9 at the Coca-Cola Dome for the Celebrate Africa FIFA World Cup event, which I am very thankful for and very excited about. My new album,* Sand & Water, *is doing very well, and I am still touring all over South Africa promoting it. I am also working on a second duet album with Dozi, which is due for release at the end of 2010. Oh yes! And I'm going to make some time for myself as well!*

Sometimes we just need to shift our focus to put things into perspective and see clearly again.

I know that other people's experiences and needs may be different from mine, including requiring medical intervention; everyone's body chemistry is different. If you need conventional medical treatment, don't feel discouraged from seeking it.

MY SOUL

You are not a human being in search of a spiritual experience.
You are a spiritual being immersed in a human experience.

– PIERRE TEILHARD DE CHARDIN

We forget this as soon as we arrive, and it often takes us a lifetime to remember it again. There is a spiritual answer to every question, but we search for answers in the physical. This always leads to more questions and leaves us feeling confused, unsatisfied, scared, guilty, lost, and alone.

I know that I have disengaged myself from the Oneness that we are all part of when I experience these feelings, and I then go within to find peace. To know that I am part of and one with everyone and everything around me, as well as with my Creator, is enough.

MY FAITH

I have faith in God and I have faith in unconditional love. What I believe will shine through my being. Words can never do it justice.

SOUL SOARING

My soul soars when I engage with my Creator, and I then experience His Spirit in everything: the smell of a beautiful red rose, the laughter of a child, a light breeze through the leaves of a willow tree, a smile from a stranger, the caring eyes of a mother, the protective arms of a father, a hug between friends, an understanding glance between husband and wife, a kind word, and a positive thought. To soar, I must remember who I am and understand that I am part of everything—one with it all. By being engaged in this way, I can experience soul soaring on a daily basis.

I have faith in God and I have faith in unconditional love.

My song "Soul's Lullaby" is another example of where I've used vocal sounds, instead of words, with the melody that came to me.

SOUL'S LULLABY

Touch the fragile heart
Caress the secrets it won't show
Gently guide the troubled soul
And show it where to go

Understand the loneliness as if it were your own
Share the love you feel, for love will change the world we know

Su le Cara Te le Se Ra Hush now, weary one
Surrender to the light, surrender to the light

Laugh into the sunlight, it's inviting you to stay
Listen to the silence, let it drown the noise away

Su le Cara Te le Se Ra Hush now, weary one
Surrender to the light, surrender to the light
Touch the fragile heart
Caress the secrets it won't show
Gently guide the troubled soul
And show it where to go ...

CHAPTER FOUR

RECONNECTING RELATIONSHIPS

I have often wondered what it would be like if it were just me, here on Earth on my own. What would I do? How would I be? Even as an introvert who needs to be on her own to recharge, I have learned that we cannot develop, grow, or even survive without other human beings around us.

Can you imagine having no one to talk to, to love, to be with, or to grow old with? What would be the point of living?

We are all soundboards for each other and play a vital part in each other's growth and learning processes.

Things that frustrate, irritate, or annoy us about other people are usually the things we are guilty of ourselves; others merely reflect what is within us, which is why we notice them in the first place. One of my favorite quotes is "If you spot it, you've got it!"

My life coach, Hanna Kok, taught me when I'm pointing a finger at someone to always look at the three fingers pointing back at me. It's a very annoying exercise, but I must admit, it's very effective.

> *If you spot it, you've got it!*

We cannot change others, no matter how hard we try; we can only change ourselves. When we are confronted with difficult people, we have to ask ourselves what we can learn from them and how we can grow from our experience.

The way we respond to the people around us is also a reflection of how we love ourselves. I am sometimes confronted with inconsiderate people. Applying the

> *We cannot change others, no matter how hard we try; we can only change ourselves.*

"three fingers pointing back" rule, I have to ask myself, "Where am I being inconsiderate?"

It turns out that I am incredibly inconsiderate toward myself. I don't allow myself enough rest, I try to take responsibility for other people's lives, and I haven't learned to say "no" or set boundaries. Now, when I experience people as inconsiderate, I immediately look within and sort myself out first. It's amazing how seldom inconsiderate people bother me when I am considerate toward myself.

There are many different kinds of relationships, all of which help us to know and understand ourselves a little better. We need to know and understand ourselves if we want to grow spiritually, or even just live blissfully.

Relationships become complicated when we are unaware of who we are and why we react the way we do. It's a bit of a catch-22, actually. We need relationships to know and understand ourselves, but without knowing and understanding ourselves, relationships are really difficult. That is why our relationships with our parents are often the hardest; they are, after all, our very first relationships here on Earth.

PARENTS

I believe that if we cannot eventually come to a place where we can accept, forgive if necessary, and love our parents unconditionally, we will continue to be confronted with the lessons we have failed to learn from them.

It is not what our parents did, or did not do, that will determine the end result of our lives, but how we deal, and continue to deal, with it. It is completely up to us to decide how much we will allow our childhood experiences to influence our lives.

You often hear stories about children from the same household who were treated the same way, yet one makes a success of his or her life, while the other one doesn't. It's a decision. You can decide to use your experiences to your advantage or disadvantage; it's really that simple! When we excuse ourselves from taking responsibility for our own lives and blame others when things aren't working out for us, we only complicate things for ourselves. If we do that, we will always be victims. I decided long ago that I was not going to be a victim in this world.

Just last night I answered an e-mail from one of my supporters, asking me for some advice. She is currently taking classes in composition, and feels that her father doesn't support her passion and dream to write music. He just wants her to "finish with the songwriting stuff" so she can focus on more important things. I replied to her, telling her that my own father once told me to forget the idea of becoming a star. He only told me this because he loves me and the last thing he wanted was for me to be hurt. That was his way of trying to protect me and save me from disappointment.

I could easily have chosen to set my father's mind at ease and done something safe instead, something less challenging … but I would probably have ended up doing something I hated and then blamed him for my unhappiness. It was my life and I wanted to sing and write songs. I knew it wouldn't be an easy career, but I had made the choice, so I also had to carry the consequences, which I did. When things became really bad for me financially, I didn't ask my parents to bail me out; I made a plan and bailed myself out.

I would not have been the person I am today, had it not been for my parents' weaknesses as well as their strengths.

Although I have wonderful parents, I also had issues with them, as most children do. I am deeply grateful for those issues because I would not have been the person I am today had it not been for my parents' weaknesses as well as their strengths.

I have spent a lot of time dealing with those issues, but letting go and forgiving became a lot easier when I took the time to get to know my parents.

In Louise Hay's *Love Yourself, Heal Your Life Workbook,* she says:

We are all victims of victims, and [your parents] could not teach you something that they did not know. If your mother or father did not know how to love themselves, it would have been impossible for them to teach you how to love yourself. They were coping as best they could with the information they had. Think for a minute about how they were raised. If you want to understand your parents more, I suggest that you ask them about their childhoods.

Listen not only to *what* they are telling you, but notice what happens to them *while* they are speaking. What is their body language like? Can they make *eye* contact with you? Look into their eyes and *see* if you can find their inner child. You may only see it for a split second, but it may reveal some valuable information.[1]

Louise Hay, a well-known self-help author, grew up in poverty and was battered and abused during her childhood, but she turned it all around for herself by releasing negative beliefs and changing the way she thought. Today she no longer lives in pain and suffering, but has created a wonderful life for herself as someone who is known for helping others.

> *The most important thing my parents did for me was to accept and love me just the way I am.*

I have met my parents' "inner children," and I only hope that one day my children will take the time to meet mine. What I admire most about my parents now is how they've grown over the years. They are not afraid to admit when they are wrong, and they have the courage and willingness to work on their weaknesses.

The most important thing my parents did for me was to accept and love me just the way I am, and I am forever grateful for that. I wish I had noticed this when I was still a child, but I suppose that is all part of growing up.

SIBLINGS

Our relationships with our parents and siblings help us prepare for the big wide world out there. Siblings usually present a whole new and different set of challenges. Suddenly we have to share; sometimes we have to take care of them (or they have to take care of us). We may be compared with them or compare ourselves with them. We might have to deal with a much stronger or weaker personality. We may be so similar that establishing our own identity becomes a challenge, or so different that relating to each other is difficult. When we throw parents into that mix of new challenges, we have a nice stew. Whether it brews to perfection or destruction is our choice.

I am the eldest of three daughters. My middle sister is a year and a half younger than I am, and the youngest is ten years my junior. As the firstborn, I was often put in charge of the others. This was a good thing because I learned to take responsibility from an early age, but later on, I learned that I also needed to let other people take responsibility for their own lives. When we allow ourselves to be a crutch for others, we don't give them the chance to heal; plus we have a heavy load to bear, which can leave us feeling resentful.

> *When we allow ourselves to be a crutch for others, we don't give them the chance to heal.*

As with our parents, if we cannot eventually come to a place where we can accept, forgive if necessary, and love our siblings unconditionally, we will continue to be confronted with those same lessons we have failed to learn from them. As a child and young adult, I was mainly focused on myself and my dreams, and because of that, I was always too busy to spend time with my sisters. In my case, I had to forgive myself for sometimes pushing my sisters away from me instead of including them in my life. Thankfully, my sisters forgave me, and that made it easier for me to forgive myself. My sisters taught me a lot about myself, and I love them very much for that, but also because they are two beautiful women whom I admire. I am thankful that they love and accept me just the way I am.

FRIENDS

I never really understood the importance of having friends until I was about 25 years old. Up to the age of 14, I was content in my own company, but when I developed an interest in the opposite sex, I started to allow my boyfriend at the time into my life. In high school, I dated a few boys from our neighboring school, because the boys in my school never asked me out. I met my first serious boyfriend at 16, and we were together for six years, but when I went to study music in South Africa, he stayed in Namibia, so things didn't work out. I was engaged to my next great love; we had been together for four years when he broke our engagement and left me for someone else. I was devastated and I thought I was going to die! Suddenly I realized that I was alone in Johannesburg with no friends and no money because I had just quit my teaching job. My mother suggested that I return home, but I knew that would be a step backward, so I decided to stay and brave the unknown.

Rejection is very painful, and when someone you love leaves you for someone else, the first thing you do is wonder what is wrong with you. Suddenly you feel unattractive, unwanted, and scared. What if no one will ever love you again?

One night I ran into an old acquaintance of mine from the Pretoria Technikon, where we had studied music together. I told him my whole heartbreaking story, and I will never forget the way he just sat there, crying with me. It was a very special moment. I had never realized what a friend I had in him until I needed a friend. He is still one of my dearest and oldest friends today. Not long after that, I cried with him when his first wife left him for someone else.

I am relatively new at establishing friendships since I only started at 25, and I still have a lot to learn, but one thing I do know now is that having friends is very important. Friends should be honest with each other, with unconditional love—not in a way that makes the other person feel judged or unloved. For instance, when I asked my dear friend if I still looked great in my bikini, he told me that I had looked better. Had he lied and said that I looked great, I would probably have continued to put on weight, because I was lying to myself at that stage.

> *It is important for us to be honest with ourselves if we want to make our friendships work.*

We usually know the answers to our questions already, but we ask others, secretly hoping they will lie to us and make us feel better about ourselves. It is important for us to be honest with ourselves if we want to make our friendships work.

There are many different kinds of friendship. Some friends are in our lives for a short while, some for a lifetime, and others for a few seconds. I believe that anyone who teaches me something about myself is a friend. We have friends we party with, soul friends, friends we work with, friends we meet in a crisis, friends in a shared sport or hobby, and friends from our school days. The list goes on, and I think it's amazing. I used to think friendship was about spending a lot of time with someone, remembering important dates like birthdays, sharing things, or giving each other things. Based on that model, I rate very poorly. Every time I meet a potential friend, I warn them that I am not very good at friendship, but thankfully my friends have accepted and loved me just the way I am.

> *I believe that anyone who teaches me something about myself is a friend.*

I have been blessed with amazing friends, and I have learned a great deal from them. One of my dearest friends has even become part of our family to help us with all our responsibilities, and because of her love and acceptance I am convinced that angels move among us.

ROMANTIC LIFE PARTNERS

I think one of the things I love most about my husband is his sense of humor and ability to make me laugh. One day we had an argument—yes, we argue, but we usually make up fairly quickly. We're not really the sulking, "cold war" types, we're more of the "thunderstorm and then it's all over and forgotten" types. On this particular day, however, I locked myself in our bedroom and refused to open the door, just to let him know that I was really upset. We had a big room with a smaller room adjacent to it, where I started working on my computer and totally forgot about him. Suddenly he just appeared out of nowhere, grinning and very full of himself. Surprised, I asked him how he had broken into the room, and he announced very proudly, "Through the roof!" That made me forget why I was angry; I just burst out laughing and all was forgiven.

In my view, your relationship with your life partner is definitely one of the hardest and most challenging. There are many reasons why, but I think the main one is that we expect so much. I am sure that every one of us could fill a book if we wrote down a list of the expectations we have of our partners. We expect to be loved, desired, respected, appreciated, romanced, understood, and forgiven, just to name a few—and if our partner doesn't live up to our expectations, the relationship becomes heavy with problems. I believe that it is these expectations that usually leave us feeling disappointed and unsatisfied. I have experienced this many times, but it only really hit me a few days ago.

It is expectations that usually leave us feeling disappointed and unsatisfied.

As I write this, it is January 2, 2011, and every year I make a New Year's resolution to work harder on my marriage and spend more time with my husband, because he is, after all, the love of my life and the most important person on this earth to me. Year after year I feel that I have failed at this, and this year I asked myself, "Why is it so hard?" The minute the pressure is on (which, in our lives, is quite often with triplets, a high profile, and our stressful jobs), instead of having each other's backs, we're at each other's throats! I realized that I expect too much from this wonderful husband of mine, and when he does fail, I focus only on that and forget about all the amazing things he contributes. I was so focused on him that I hadn't realized I was guilty of everything I had accused him of. I need to treat him with love and respect if I want to be treated with love and respect … if I want him to make me feel desired, I have to make him feel desired.

This counts for every expectation I have, and vice versa. You see, what we want, we have to give, and what we give, we shall receive. The trick is knowing that it starts with me. I can't wait for him to do it first and then follow—"When you're nice to

The trick is knowing that it starts with me.

me, I will be nice to you" or "If you treat me with respect, I will be more loving," etc. This is just a vicious, never-ending circle of punishment that will never be resolved.

Now let's take this a step further: How about giving without expecting anything in return? After all, isn't that what unconditional love is about? I decided to start loving my husband the way I would like to be loved, without expecting anything in return. There was an immediate change in our relationship, and I already feel so much more love for him and from him. I know it's still going to be a challenge, but I just need to constantly remind myself not to expect anything and to give what I desire.

The "three fingers pointing back" theory works wonders in a marriage because if something irritates or bothers you about your partner, you are most probably also guilty of it in some form or another. Nobody owes us anything, so it's not fair to think that our life partners owe us something. When we lay expectations on others, they become nervous under the pressure and then usually just end up letting us down.

So what if I have no expectations and I love unconditionally, but my life partner treats me badly anyway? We cannot change anyone but ourselves. Focus on your side of the relationship by loving yourself, and then make decisions based on what is going to bring out the best in you and be the best for you. If you are unhappy, you won't be able to make anyone else happy. Your life will be exactly as you've chosen it to be, so choose well.

Your life will be exactly as you've chosen it to be, so choose well.

HAVE FAITH

Sometimes it feels like we're strangers
Although I know you well
At times I can't help feeling lonely
Even though you're here with me

We see things differently
Baby, you and me
I know that it's hard on you
But know that it's hard on me, too

So we've got to have faith in us
I've got to have faith in you
If we want to see this through
I've got to have faith in you
We've got to have faith in us
You've got to have faith in me
Nothing good comes easily
So, baby, have faith in me
Nothing good comes easily
So, baby, you've got to have
Have some faith in me

Sometimes I look at you and wonder
Why you do the things you do
But in the end it doesn't matter
You do what you believe is true

We see things differently
Baby, you and me
I know that it's hard on you
But know that it's hard on me, too

So we've got to have faith in us
I've got to have faith in you
If we want to see this through
I've got to have faith in you
We've got to have faith in us
You've got to have faith in me
Nothing good comes easily
So, baby, have faith in me
Nothing good comes easily
So, baby, you've got to have
Have some faith in me

CHILDREN

I love children. I always feel a little sorry for them, though, probably because my own childhood was very difficult for me. I couldn't wait to grow up and become an adult, and I must say I have never missed being a child. Children are so vulnerable; we should love and protect them to the best of our ability.

If we were not protected or loved as children, we often end up repeating the behaviors we were subjected to. It is possible to break that chain, but only if we can forgive those who harmed us, heal ourselves, and unconditionally accept and love ourselves.

Not long ago, I performed at a big "Carols by Candlelight" event, and all the little children came to the front to sing with us. Looking at them, I prayed that they would be kept safe and only experience love, and then realized that was never going to happen. They will experience hurt, some more than others, because life is hard. If it were easy, we would not grow, learn, or discover who we are. So I started to pray that God would bless them with wisdom instead. May we all be blessed with the wisdom to realize that life is not about what happens to us, but how we handle the things that happen to us.

Like adults, children just want to be noticed, understood, accepted, and loved. I once put a notice up on my fridge, asking the people who work in my house to treat my children as they would want to be treated themselves. Nobody likes to be pulled or forced, especially not by someone twice your size. How would you feel if you were continuously ignored and told that you should be seen and not heard? If our children's future is important to us, we need to listen to them and treat them in a way that shows how much they matter. Sure, we will make mistakes, but those will only make our children stronger. What is important is that they always know that we love them, that they matter, and that they are very important to us.

Children must always know that we love them, that they matter and that they are very important to us.

COLLEAGUES

One of my favorite things about being a performing artist is the fact that it gives me the opportunity to work with a diverse group of wonderful people. I have worked with musicians, sound and light engineers, producers, personal assistants, agents, managers, and CEOs, and they have all played a very important part in making me into the person I am today.

I love being on the road with fellow musicians and crew members, sharing ideas and views on just about every topic under the sun. We have learned a lot from each other, and they have helped me grow tremendously. I have immensely fond memories of our time spent together and hope to continue working with many more like them.

Working with people can be challenging, though, and I have made many mistakes along the way. Sometimes I have disappointed and upset people even though it has never been my intention to hurt anyone. When I did become aware that my actions had caused someone grief, I would apologize immediately if I was wrong. Many of my mistakes were made because I was inexperienced, impatient, and indecisive, but most

We need to become aware of the consequences of our mistakes and take responsibility for them.

of all because I am human, and I am sure I will make many more. We need to make mistakes in order to learn, but most important, we need to become aware of their consequences and to take responsibility.

Everyone has a unique personality, and we all perceive and experience things differently. To work in harmony with people, we really need to try and understand how they think, and why they think like they do. We also need to know how people like to do things and why they like to do them that way. It takes time to really know and understand your colleagues, but you will be successful if you make the effort. We need to focus on each other's strengths and cover for each other if either is lacking in a certain area. The problem, however, is always our ego. When our ego takes over, the ship is bound to sink.

This reminds me of a story. The CEO of a company was in a meeting with a client when one of the company's employees suddenly stormed in, ranting and raving about some problem he had. After a while the CEO calmly told the employee to try to remember rule six. Immediately the employee calmed down, apologized, and left the office. After a while the client became very curious and asked the CEO what rule six was. The CEO replied, "Rule six is don't take yourself too seriously." The client then asked what the other rules were, to which the CEO replied, "There aren't any other rules, only rule six."

I have been in situations where I had to sit on my ego to get the job done, and today I am thankful that I managed to do that. As an entrepreneur I have learned to keep my eye on the bigger picture and not jeopardize the desired end result by focusing on petty issues. I also try not to make emotional decisions or react emotionally in business, although this is not an easy task.

I have learned to team up with people who are strong in the areas in which I am not. In this way I strengthen my business and also eliminate unnecessary pressure for myself. For example, I have never really had a great sense of style and have no idea which brands are hot and which aren't … I wouldn't even know it if I were wearing a great brand. Although I liked to dress up in my childhood, I now prefer walking around in my jeans and T-shirts when I'm not working or performing. Unfortunately for me, I am in the public eye and what I wear is noticed. I do, however, have a talent for spotting talent in others, so early in my career, I started relying on talented designers and stylists to guide me in that department. Thanks to their help and guidance, *Die Rapport* (a South African newspaper) awarded me third place on their list of ten best-dressed women of 2010. Even though receiving third place had nothing to do with my own fashion sense, I felt pleased with myself for having chosen the right people to dress me.

> *I have also learned to team up with people who are strong in the areas in which I am not.*

When it comes to working with people, I've realized that knowing myself and understanding others are the keys to successful working relationships—that, and rule six!

FELLOW HUMAN BEINGS

Why do we find it so hard to accept and respect anything that is different from what we know? Not everyone can think, believe, look, or act in the same way. We all have our unique differences, but we are also very similar. Even though our culture, language, color, and religion may differ, we all cry when we are sad, laugh when we are happy, and long for only one thing: to love and to be loved.

The need to protect our way and our truth—to fight for what we believe is right or for what we believe is ours—stems from fear. We fear the unknown; we fear what we are not used to, and we fear what we don't understand, but most of all, we fear what we think we might lose. In the end, it is always either our ego, which is the false self, or our greed that makes us experience fear.

Acting out of fear leads to fighting, which usually ends up in war and separation. We remain blissfully unaware of the fact that fear has been used through the ages to gain power over us. If we cannot confront our fear, face it, under-

> *Love cannot be where fear is present.*

stand it, and take control of it, we will continue to allow it to rule our lives, and love cannot be where fear is present. We spend so much energy on fighting instead of loving that it can only leave us feeling exhausted, empty, and unhappy. Feeling this way doesn't serve us or the world in any way, but we still continue convincing ourselves that our fight is a worthy one.

I believe there is enough space in this world for all the different cultures, languages, colors, and religions. Our ego, however, wants us to believe that we are superior to those who are different from us. We tell ourselves that our way and what we believe is the only truth and the only way, and dedicate our lives to convincing others to see things our way. If we do not succeed, we just separate ourselves from each other. The more we separate ourselves from each other, the more afraid and alone we become. Accepting and knowing that we are all created by our Creator and that we are all part of and one with the Source of creation will inspire us to embrace each other with compassion, acceptance, respect, and love.

Dr. Wayne Dyer suggests that we ask for Divine assistance, and not beseech God to help us defeat others in any way during our private, quiet, prayerful moments. Instead, we might pray like this: "Dear God, make me an instrument of Thy love. I want to be like You. I have forgiven them, and I have forgiven myself."[2]

HEY YOU

Hey you, yes you
You think you're all alone out there
And no one understands you

Hey you, yes you
Stop thinking you're alone out there
And no one ever sees you

If you feel the world is closing down on you
And no one really cares
And you see that time has passed you by
And you feel there's no real love out there
You're wrong, just be strong
'Cause somewhere you'll find a place,
Somewhere you'll find a place where you belong

Hey you, yes you
Somewhere high above the stars
There's someone smiling down on you

If you feel the world is closing down on you
And no one really cares
And you see that time has passed you by
And you feel there's no real love out there
You're wrong, just be strong
'Cause somewhere you'll find a place,
Somewhere you'll find a place where you belong

CHAPTER FIVE

THE MIRACLE
OF THREE

Have you ever bought something you thought was quite rare, something you've never really noticed before, and then suddenly it's everywhere?

Well, I had never seen triplets before I had my own, but then I suddenly started noticing them everywhere! Being in the public eye helped: When people heard I was expecting triplets, I was contacted by a number of moms of triplets, and I am often introduced to triplets at shows, which is wonderful. I've met parents who have had three and sometimes even four children before they were blessed with triplets. I also met a woman who had identical triplets, which is extremely rare—something that only happens once in every 500,000 births. One night, I met a couple with 25-year-old triplets who had not known they were expecting three babies (back in those days they didn't have ultrasound) and thought they were going to have one really big baby! Imagine their surprise when she went into natural labor and three babies were born. Did I mention *natural* labor?! They told me that they had eventually asked the doctor to put out the lights, please, since that was obviously what was attracting them all. I am lucky to have known that I was expecting triplets from the start.

I am very grateful for this constant reminder that life is a miracle and also for the support from other mothers in the same situation; it's good to know that there are people with some experience out there that I can call if I ever find myself in a situation that I don't know how to handle.

PREPARE AND PLAN

When I discovered we were expecting triplets, I prepared myself as though a tsunami was going to hit. I read every book I could find, and we attended classes on every baby topic you can think of. I knew our babies were going to be premature, so we visited the neonatal unit prior to their birth, and this prepared us for the six weeks they had to spend there. It must be a terrible shock to have a premature baby unexpectedly, and I was extremely thankful for the chance to prepare myself.

I will never forget the third day that we had our three babies back from the hospital. They were like tiny little skeletons: Tayden, the singleton, weighed in at about 4.4 pounds, with identical twins Jade and Kaeley just below that number. They were terribly fragile and looked so similar that it was hard to tell them apart. We hadn't slept in two days, so we were overtired and having trouble focusing. We didn't realize that we had accidentally fed one of them twice until she started throwing up.

The thing we learned about triplets that day was that if one throws up, the others will soon follow ... it's like a chain reaction. Soon they were all throwing up and crying. It was chaos!

The moment was just too big for us, and my husband and I broke down sobbing on the nursery floor. We were so afraid that we might be killing our babies. There were just so many of them, and we had never done this before. We sat there holding each other and crying for a while, and then I knew something had to be done about the situation if we were ever going to survive. We needed structure, we needed a plan, but first we needed sleep. Nobody can function without sleep.

A dear friend came to help us out so that we could have some rest that night, and when I woke up a few hours later, I went on a mission to plan things thoroughly. I asked one of our two nannies to do night shifts; that way, only one of us would need to wake up while the other slept. We also did shifts; I would stay up till 3 A.M. and my husband would take the late morning shift, or vice versa. Next, I painted the pinkie nail of one of the identical twins red to help us with identification. We still mixed them up occasionally and sometimes put one of them in the wrong cot, but we've never fed any of them twice again. Finally I bought them each a little book in which we logged their feeds, diaper changes, and naps.

We needed to keep track of how much milk they drank to make sure they each had enough. We also needed to know if someone didn't poo so that we could stay on top of aches, pains, and possible infections. Keeping track of these things is vital with premature babies, and their little books helped considerably. From that day on, we ran things like an army camp. Everyone had strict orders, and no one was allowed to deviate from the plan. Every four hours I would express milk while the girls were sleeping. When they woke up, we would change their diapers, play with them for a while, and feed them. We quickly figured out how one person could feed all three of them at once: We would make them sit in their little car seats and fold one of those big old white material diapers under their bottles to hold them in place. Then we would burp them, and soon after that they would go back to sleep, just for the whole routine to start all over again. It was a crazy time. I constantly thought I was hearing babies crying—even while they slept. We hardly got any sleep, but we soon adjusted. It's amazing how much we can cope with when we have to.

I can honestly say that planning things properly saved our lives. Not just during their first few years, but also prior to having them.

I knew that I would have to take time off while I was pregnant. This meant that we would need to wait until I was established enough in the music industry and had enough savings to cover expenses during my maternity leave before we could proceed. My first DVD was released just before I fell pregnant, and fortunately we were able to ride on those funds for a while. I can't imagine what would have happened if we hadn't planned.

Planning things properly saved our lives.

We would have been in dire financial trouble, my career would have suffered, and all of this would definitely have put a lot of pressure on our marriage.

Having children does put strain on a marriage because they demand so much of your time. We were married for seven years before we had our girls, and I am extremely grateful that things worked out the way we planned. I believe that it's important to wait until you are ready before you have children, and also to have them for the right reasons—because you have something to give and share, not just because you think you'll get something from it. Our lives should already have meaning before we have children. We should be happy and fulfilled before bringing another being into our lives. Having children for the right reasons can make a marriage stronger and more fulfilling, but having them to save a marriage is absurd.

One evening, after putting the girls to bed, we watched a *Shrek* DVD that someone had given us at my baby shower. Right at the end of the movie, Shrek and Fiona are looking down at their three sleeping babies, and with a wicked glint in his eye, Shrek asks, "What shall we do now?" The next scene shows the two of

Our lives should already have meaning before we have children.

them passed out on their bed, fast asleep. A few seconds later, a baby starts crying. Andrew and I could relate to that completely, and we both just burst out laughing. I'm sure every new parent feels that way.

When we fell pregnant, we had just finished paying off a 4x4 that we were planning to take on a trip through Namibia—my husband's dream holiday. We were still waiting for the car to arrive (there was a very long waiting list for that specific model) when we received the news that we were expecting triplets. We canceled the car and the trip, and used the refund to build on some now badly needed extra rooms. We can always do our trip later; it will be more fun having our three little girls with us anyway. Plans often need to be changed, adapted, and reconsidered. I am just grateful that we have the ability to plan—and isn't it amazing that we can always make another plan if we have to? As the Afrikaans saying goes, "*'n boer maak 'n plan*" (a farmer makes a plan).

We also have to keep in mind that planning is just a small part of life. There are a lot of things that we cannot plan for, but being prepared for the big stuff might help us cope with the small stuff (and vice versa). We didn't plan to have three babies at once (although we had hoped for three ultimately), but being prepared for one baby made it easier to cope with the three that we were blessed with.

Isn't it amazing that we can always make another plan if we have to?

Problems arise that cannot be anticipated. For example, the girls fell ill when I started giving them cow's milk. They were about five months old at the time, and we returned home from a performance one night to find Tayden running a high fever. At that stage we were in Yzerfontein on the West Coast, more than 35 miles from the nearest hospital, so it was very late by the time we arrived. We waited quite a while before the doctor told us that he suspected meningitis and would need to admit her.

I didn't know what to do—stay with my sick child or go home to my other two children? The doctor made the decision for me and told me to go home. My husband stayed with Tayden, but it was still very hard to leave her. I finally arrived home only to find Kaeley and Jade running high fevers as well, so back to the hospital we went. They were terribly traumatized when they had to have lumbar punches to determine whether or not they had meningitis, and it was brutal listening to their screams … poor Kaeley screamed so much that it caused a hernia that still hasn't healed. They did have meningitis, but thankfully it was viral (bacterial meningitis is much more dangerous). They spent four nights in the hospital, and we stayed with them. I had to do a show on every one of those nights and prepared myself for my performances in the hospital bathroom. The hospital staff was amazing, and we were extremely grateful for the support we received during that time, although it's all a bit of a blur to me now. It continues to amaze me how much we can cope with when we have faith.

When we relocated to Johannesburg about three months later, the girls became sick again and all three were admitted to the hospital again. Fortunately, the hospital was only five minutes away from our house in Johannesburg, and this time they were only there for about two days. Nicolette, my physical trainer, suggested I change them over to goat's milk, and when I spoke to our doctor about it, he also thought it would be a good idea … apparently cow's milk contains about 18 proteins that the human body cannot digest. It was the best thing I have ever done for my children, and they haven't been back in the hospital since. Soon after that, I started adding fresh carrot, spinach, celery, and apple juice to the goat's milk, and eventually replaced it with juices entirely. They still drink about three 9-ounce bottles of it every day, and it has improved their health immensely. They love their vegetable juice and get everything they need from it, so I don't need to worry if they won't eat their greens. I am really happy about this, because every mother just wants her children to be healthy, and I know that depends mainly on what we put into our bodies.

There comes a stage when you stop panicking and start enjoying the chaos that three babies bring into your life. Imagine being one of two people changing two poo diapers with one very curious baby roaming around. You might be just in time to prevent the roamer from sticking her

There comes a stage when you stop panicking …

hands into the bum cream, but that leaves one of the others free to grab a dirty diaper and swing it around. You quickly acclimate to smells, and somehow you stop noticing the mess around you … you adapt or die. Even my poor husband (whom our nannies nicknamed "Mr. Min"—a furniture polish we use here in South Africa—because he's such a perfectionist about the house) eventually submitted to the disorder.

One day Andrew and I were busy burping the girls. I had two of them on my lap, and Andrew was holding Jade, who had started crying. Just then, his cell phone also started to ring. Being a typical man, he finds multitasking a challenge, and I could see he was stressed, so I said, "Baby, just don't answer your phone right now." He answered, "Stop screaming at me!" I guess he felt like the world was screaming at him in that moment.

I have the most amazing husband, and I couldn't have picked a better father for my children. When I was too scared to bathe them for the first time while they were still in the ICU, Andrew bathed all three of them, one by one, as if he had done it a million times before. He is "hands on" and helps with everything. During the first year with the triplets, he often dreamt that we were falling, and he would grab me in his sleep saying, "I've got you, baby, I've got you!" I don't know what I would have done without my husband, my world, my rock.

PATIENCE AND PRAYER

When babies become toddlers and start running around, you have a whole new set of problems on your hands. Two arms simply aren't enough for three toddlers, so after a while you become quite skilled at using all the other bits of your body, too. It's a very exciting but tiring time, and it becomes tempting to lose it with everyone around you. I think cultures that let the older people look after their young ones are very wise; with age comes patience. Having turned 40 this year helps me, but there are still moments when things just become too much; at that point, the only thing left to do is pray. Sometimes my nerves can't handle seeing one of them getting too close to a high edge or just missing a sharp table corner, so I shut my eyes and pray that the danger will be over when I open them again.

It must be very hard being a toddler and part of a set of triplets—trying to figure out how you should behave and where you fit in, and fighting for attention can't be easy. I try my best not to make it worse for them by losing my patience during this trying time. In toddlers' minds, everything is theirs. I really enjoyed reading "Property Law as Viewed by a Toddler" by Michael V. Hernandez:

1.   If I like it, it's mine.
2.   If it's in my hand, it's mine.
3.   If I can take it from you, it's mine.

4. If I had it a little while ago, it's mine.
5. If it's mine, it must never appear to be yours in any way.
6. If I'm doing or building something, all the pieces are mine.
7. If it looks like it's mine, it's mine.
8. If I saw it first, it's mine.
9. If I can see it, it's mine.
10. If I think it's mine, it's mine.
11. If I want it, it's mine.
12. If I need it, it's mine (yes, I know the difference between "want" and "need"!).
13. If I say it's mine, it's mine.
14. If you don't stop me from playing with it, it's mine.
15. If you tell me I can play with it, it's mine.
16. If it will upset me too much when you take it away from me, it's mine.
17. If I (think I) can play with it better than you can, it's mine.
18. If I play with it long enough, it's mine.
19. If you are playing with something and you put it down, it's mine.
20. If it's broken, it's yours (no, wait; all the pieces are mine).[1]

One night, Tayden didn't feel well and vomited on her "blanky." After cleaning everything up, I had the difficult job of explaining that her blanky was now dirty and would have to be washed before she could have it back. She didn't look very happy with this arrangement, and I was surprised that she didn't create a bigger scene, but I soon realized that she already had a plan and was just waiting for me to leave the room. We had installed some cameras in the girls' room so that we would be able to keep an eye on them at all times, and when I got back to our room, I saw her climbing straight out of her cot, running to Jade's cot, stealing Jade's blanket out from under her nose, and quickly making her way back to her own cot. I hadn't even known that Tayden could climb in and out of her cot on her own at that stage! Of course, Jade woke up and cried, but luckily their room was dark and Jade was sleepy, so she accepted a replacement blanket that was close enough to the "real blanky" and went straight back to sleep. Tayden would never have fallen for that stunt! Her perception and reasoning are exceptional. She even knew to target Jade because she would never have been able to steal Kaeley's blanket and get away with it.

In the beginning, everyone called everyone else "Kaeley," so anything that upset Tayden was "Kaeley's fault." With her sisters being identical, there were just too many Kaeleys in Tayden's life. At one point, Jade also thought she was Kaeley. I guess saying "Kaeley" was easier for her than "Jade." They even called Tayden "Kaeley" for a while. Eventually they learned their real names, although I am sure mischief will make them pretend to be each other again someday. Kaeley became so used to being the guilty party that she even got confused the other day when one of her sisters hurt her, and cried out, "Naughty Kaeley, naughty Kaeley."

They are now three and a half years old. I sometimes walk into their room and find everything (and I mean everything) on the floor. When I ask them who did it, they immediately call out each other's names, especially Tayden ... she always knows who did it, and it's never her. Only Kaeley ever admits guilt; she even owns it proudly—with a big grin! Jade will pretend to be just as angry as I am (I think she might even really be), and she will immediately sort out the mess, and her sisters, on my behalf.

Tantrums, especially when they're thrown in view of the whole world, have made us appreciate the value of staying home. Here, as with throwing up and crying, the chain reaction rule also applies, and can turn a nice enjoyable family outing into a total nightmare as three screaming toddlers run in opposite directions with just two of us to handle them. Being a public figure makes things worse. There's no way to stay in control of a situation like that, so again, the only thing to do is close your eyes and pray ... or just stay home.

They always compete for attention, and they've found some very creative ways of attracting it. Somewhere, they picked up that pain captures attention, so if all else fails, they'll come up with an "ouch" somewhere. If Andrew and I have been out, they will all run to the toy box and present us with the biggest toy they can find, instead of just running straight to us when we arrive home. They think they need something more to engage our attention for longer. They've also divided us up. Once, while we were away, Tayden told Kaeley and Jade that I belonged to her and Daddy was theirs. When the nanny told them that we both belonged to all of them, Tayden was very upset by this, and Jade went to console her, telling her that it was okay. She could have me.

They are becoming more and more caring toward each other, and they look out for each other, but there are times when they attack each other. They sometimes smack each other, pull each other's hair, and even bite. How do you discipline your children and teach them not to hit each other? Smacking them is a contradiction; in fact, I noticed after giving them a few smacks that they started disciplining each other (and us) that way, too; for instance, Jade would smack me if I had smacked Tayden for being naughty. Once Andrew gave Kaeley a smack on the bum because she was splashing everything and everyone in the bathroom, and before we knew what was happening, everyone was smacking everyone. We just burst out laughing and realized that there are times when this form of discipline does not work. They even started using objects to hit each other at one stage, after which they would say, "Naughty, naughty teddy" (or whatever they had used). I thought it was very creative of them at first, but when the objects became bigger and heavier, it had to stop.

They all respond to different forms of discipline. At one point I tried making them stand in the corner, but Jade would happily join in—in fact, I think she would easily pay me to make her stand in the corner, so needless to say, that doesn't work for her. Kaeley just laughs at a spanking, while Tayden will behave even if you just threaten her with one. It's a challenge to find out what works, and disciplining them is very painful for us, but I know that they will be the ones who suffer later in life if I don't do it now. We all need discipline; with discipline comes freedom.

One day we were walking next to the beach, and I noticed Kaeley squashing little snails on the road with her foot. I explained to her that she shouldn't do that because she was hurting the little snails and making them cry, and told her to say

We all need discipline; with discipline comes freedom.

sorry. She said, "Sorry, snail." I couldn't believe it when she proceeded to squash the very next one she saw, saying "Sorry, snail" again. They still think that apologizing makes everything right. It's going to take some time before they understand that there are consequences for their actions and that they need to take responsibility for them.

We had the biggest scare of our lives a while ago when we went to a restaurant in a mall one morning. The girls were playing happily in the play area, and I left them with the nanny there for about two minutes to take a sip of my coffee at our table. Mine were the only children in there, so I thought the nanny would be able to handle them, but when I returned, both Kaeley and Jade were missing. They had apparently slipped out through the smoking section next to the playroom, which is why we hadn't seen them coming past us. I quickly grabbed Tayden in my arms and ran into the restaurant to tell Andrew that they had gone missing and to look for them. I couldn't find them in the restaurant, so I ran outside, alerted security, and then started running wildly around the mall (which, at that point, felt enormous) looking for them and asking everyone if they had seen our little girls.

The staff at the restaurant and another man who had seen them running out of the restaurant were great and helped us look. I thought I was going to lose my mind. I just wanted to scream for my girls to hear me. Finally one of the security guards told me they had been found and were with their father. I ran toward the security room and there, head and shoulders above the crowd, coming toward me, was Andrew with our two little girls in his arms. They ran to me and I just sat down on the floor and held them, sobbing.

God gently reminded me that anger will only add to the hurt the world is already experiencing ...

They were very surprised to see me crying; they hadn't realized their fun adventure would cause us a near nervous breakdown. When Andrew had walked into the security room, they had stood there happily and said, "Hello, Daddy!" I know my tears affected them because Jade also started crying, and all three of them kissed and hugged me and stroked my hair with the greatest concern and compassion. I explained to them that they had made me very sad by running away from us and they must never do that again.

Those were the longest 15 minutes of my life. That night I was still in a state, crying every time I thought of them lost out there in the big, cruel world. I felt really angry with the world that night—for all the pain out there—but God gently reminded me that anger would only add to the hurt the world is already experiencing; I should love, because only love will help to heal it.

PARENTING

A healthy state of mind, a sense of well-being, and a good quality of life are very important when raising children. If we're unhappy, tired, negative, ill, or depressed, we can't be patient and kind. It is best for our children when we're in a good state of mind—positive, happy, rested, joyful, and full of energy. To achieve this, we need to look after ourselves first. As they say on airplane flights, "put your own oxygen mask on before helping children or anybody else." In a nutshell, to be a great parent, you need to be a great you!

To be a great parent, you need to be a great you!

There's only one lesson I really want to teach my children, and that is to love themselves. I know if they do this, it will automatically circle out and back in again, and that is my wish for them: to love and to be loved. Actions speak so much louder than words, and I know that I will turn blue in the face before my children hear anything I say to them. They will only hear what they see, so if I want them to love themselves, I must love myself.

> *We should try and be the kind of people we want our children to become.*

At the end of the day, the way we feel about ourselves and others, and the way we treat ourselves and others, will be the example our children follow. We should try to be the kind of people we want our children to become. While we are certain to make mistakes, our children will hopefully respect the fact that we continued to work on loving ourselves unconditionally because we wanted to be better parents for them.

PLEASE

"Please, dear God, protect and keep my children safe from any harm. Let them be healthy and strong, dear God; bless them with your love, your joy, and your peace, and always keep them in your loving arms."

Having my children in jeopardy is my greatest fear; however, I know fear will not help me. I need to let go of my fear and learn to trust, because my best is all I can do to protect them and keep them safe.

Last year was a terrible year for Antoinette and Wouter van der Sandt, a couple from Brits, South Africa, who lost all four of their daughters (a nine-year-old, an eight-year-old, and 4-year-old twins) in a car accident. How do you carry on after something like that has happened to you? Not only did Antoinette lose all her children, but she also sustained serious injuries and couldn't even attend their funeral. When I heard what had happened to them, I felt a huge urge to comfort them, and at the same time I prayed that nothing like that would ever happen to me. I can't imagine having to lose one child, never mind all my children. As I struggled with the fear that entered my heart, a song came to me. At first I didn't want to write it; I didn't want to go there, to where I had to try to put myself in Antoinette's position and imagine what she must feel like. Even living the experience in my mind so that I could capture it in song was overwhelming for me … how much worse must the reality of it have been? It took me two long, emotional months to write this song. The lyrics came to me while I stroked my own children's hair, put them to bed, and played with them, and all the time I kept wondering why things like this have to happen. I called the song "Until I'm Home."

Some time after I started performing the song, I received an e-mail from Antoinette thanking me for it and telling me how much it would have meant to her girls because they just loved music so much. I was incredibly moved when I heard from her. At first I didn't know how to reply. Imagine my surprise when I received a second e-mail from her, wishing me and my family a blessed Easter. Where did she find the strength to think about me during this painful time? Suddenly it became clear to me—life is not about what happens to us, but how we handle it. How we stand up after we fall, how we take responsibility for our mistakes and failures, how we continue after losing everything. Do we choose to learn from the experience, do we allow it to make us stronger, wiser people, or do we give it the power to turn our lives into a constant misery?

> *Life is not about what happens to us, but how we handle it.*

Life doesn't stop when something bad happens to us. People will grieve with us for a while, but eventually they will carry on with their own lives. It seems almost cruel when you look at it from a physical point of view, but from a spiritual perspective, life continues; it's never ending. The spirit continues when we leave our physical form. I find this very comforting, and it's wonderful to know that our loved ones continue to live with God, although we might not see them here with us. In the end, it all boils down to how we continue to live without them. I asked Antoinette if she would be willing to share her experience with us. Here is her story:

I don't believe my story has a beginning or an end. I can't remember anything about the accident; all I know is what I have been told by others. Serious injuries kept me in the ICU for nine days. I was heavily sedated to help me cope with the pain, and I spent another three weeks in a private room after that. Hundreds of people came to visit me—family and friends whom I hadn't seen in years. I really did appreciate all the visits, but sometimes, although I knew it was probably not very nice of me, I couldn't help thinking, "Wow, does it really take a near-death experience to make people come and visit?" Miranda, Marissa, Lynette, and Estelle were my everything; my life. They told me they were gone while I was in the ICU, but I don't think I believed it. Wouter had to make the decision to switch off Estelle's life support because she was already brain-dead. If I'd had to make that decision, I would not have been able to give the go-ahead; Estelle would still be lying in hospital today while I desperately held on to the hope that a miracle might happen. I don't know if I will ever be able to find closure because I couldn't attend their funeral.

I am precious about their graves; I cut the grass myself twice a week, and every Sunday, Wouter and I put fresh flowers down. I even obtained permission from the Department of Agriculture to plant trees, and I am so proud of how beautiful it looks there. My children were earth children. They didn't need many toys because they always played outside. They were happy being in nature. The other day, I asked my niece what she missed most about them and she said, "The original games they used to come up with."

Miranda and Marissa received their South African colors (chosen to represent South Africa in their age group) in hip-hop and modern dancing three weeks prior to the accident, and the twins wanted to play rugby when they went to primary school. They were a busy bunch.

Our house is silent now, and sometimes it feels like we're only breathing to create some movement. Since I came home from the hospital, I have kept a candle burning in our house 24 hours a day. I have kept their rooms as they were; I think I am afraid to lose their smell, because you can still smell them, especially when you open their cupboards. I open their blinds every morning, close them every night, and wash their bedding regularly.

Wouter and I have been through some rough times, but things are slowly becoming better between us now. He can't talk about it, while I just want to talk about our little girls all the time. Men and women handle trauma so differently. We have to get to know each other all over again.

Some days I just can't get up. Sleeping pills are my sanctuary when I just don't want to feel anymore. I often sleepwalk; I think I am looking for my children. Twice I have sat with a pistol in my hands and then realized, "I might never see them again if I do this." Every time I have to go for another foot operation I feel like it's my punishment for still being here while they are not. I know it's not like that, but that is how I feel. I had a light stroke two weeks ago; they say it's broken heart syndrome.

I have been to three different psychologists, but I'm afraid it's not for me. I have an amazing friend who has been carrying me since day one. She has convinced me to carry on many times when all I wanted was to give up. I also have a huge support group, and my three sisters have picked me up numerous times after I have fallen. I also have a wonderful boss; any other boss would have fired me long ago.

I think I might have been very selfish in my sorrow because I have never considered the pain that grandparents, nephews, nieces, and the rest of the family were going through. I know I will still fall many times, but I will stand up again. I will stand up for Wouter and for my family.

I try so hard to live right, but some days I feel so angry with God when I see how some mothers treat their children while mine were taken away from me. One day I will make peace with Him. I talk to Him a lot and fight just as much. Nothing and no one can replace your children; they are just such an incredible part of your life. I taught our children that you don't go to church one day a week to look for God; you have to see Him every day, in everything. God gave us our talents and everything that is beautiful. He is in everything, in every tree and every flower.

No person's pain is the same. One person can lose a dog and mourn for months because that doggy was their life. I don't know how long it takes to get over something like this, but I believe only time will heal it. Just getting up each day feels like a great milestone to me.

I must be honest—we might never understand the purpose of everything in this lifetime. Maybe one day we will, but one day just feels really far away right now. I know this accident touched many lives … we even received letters from Tanzania.

What have I learned from all of this? I have learned to look at people differently. Our lives are such a rush that we sometimes forget to notice the person next to us. I see the mistakes people make, but it's not my place to tell them, "Life is so short; what if you don't have another chance to make it right?" I wish people just wanted to see each other for what and who we really are. God gave all of us love, respect, and empathy for free; if only we could realize that. I hope my story will help you to convince people that love can never be replaced by anything.

Antoinette had been praying to God to let her see her little girls one last time. A few weeks after sending me her story, she had a wonderful dream. She was at her children's graves. It had been raining heavily the previous day and the graves had caved in. When she looked into the hole, she saw a small gift wrapped in pink paper. She bent down to pick it up and saw her little girl's hair sticking out of the ground, so she started to dig deeper. Suddenly one of her girls said, "Hello, Mamma," and less than a minute later, they were all there with her. They looked younger than they had before the accident, and she even saw that one of them had a scar on her head, although she had not seen them after the accident. They played together for

When we play, we teach our children to enjoy life.

a long time, and then they told her that they had to go and everything became quiet. An amazing peace came over her, and she felt deeply thankful for being able to see her girls again. She says she knows the hurt will never go away, but God answered her prayers and let her know that they are safe.

I am so thankful that Antoinette was willing to share her story with us. May we all be inspired to notice each other and treat each other with love, respect, and empathy. I have now changed my prayers to this: "Dear God, thank you for the strength and wisdom to deal with whatever happens in my life until I'm home."

UNTIL I'M HOME

Listen, can you hear it, there's an angel whispering your name.
A new life has begun now, but my love for you will stay the same

We were so lucky to have known you even for a while.
Lucky that you chose us, that you've blessed us with your lovely smile

How I wish that I could see you once more,
How I long to hold you in my arms.
Stroke your hair before I kiss you gently,
Lay you down to sleep just one more time.

I'll hear your laughter, I'll remember how we used to play
And I'll cherish the memory until I'm home with you one day.

Forgive me if I'm not strong, it's so hard to know I must go on,
But I know that I'm here now and for now this is where I belong

And if I could hear you, I imagine this is what you'd say,
You'd tell me not to worry, to let go, and know that you're okay.

How I wish that I could see you once more,
How I long to hold you in my arms.
Stroke your hair before I kiss you gently,
Lay you down to sleep just one more time.

I'll hear your laughter, I'll remember how we used to play
And I'll cherish the memory until I'm home with you one day

PLAY

If we can grow past our fears, past all the "dos and don'ts," past the comparing and evaluating, and past the weight we place on our own shoulders, we can enjoy playing with our children and stay young.

Play while they still want to play with us, play because we love and deserve to have fun. When we play, we teach our children to enjoy life. We show them we're alive and not just surviving. Turn everything into a game—cooking, cleaning— because life is too short to say: "Not now; later."

CHAPTER SIX

WHAT IS LOVE?

Have you ever Googled "love"? I did. It gave me such a giggle!
The first site I found was a love calculator where you could type in two names for an instantaneous result!
This was the calculation for my husband and me:

Andrew Vaughan Thompson
Sonia Aletta Nel (my birth name)
Result: 22 percent
Dr. Love thinks a relationship might work out between Andrew Vaughan Thompson and Sonia Aletta Nel, but the chance is very small. A successful relationship is possible, but you both have to work on it. Do not sit back and think that it will all work out fine, because it might not be working out the way you wanted it to. Spend as much time with each other as possible. Again, the chance of this relationship working out is very small, so even when you do work hard on it, it still might not work out.

I entered a few more names just to see what would come up; there were different predictions for each couple, but the same advice came through every time: "Talk to each other and spend time together."

This is good advice, but you'll never find the answers you're looking for from a love calculator.

So what is love?

I've decided to find out what the people of South Africa say:

SOUTH AFRICAN CELEBRITIES

Nelson Mandela (in a letter to Winnie Madikizela-Mandela, July 1, 1979): "The world is truly round and seems to start and end with those we love."

Claire Johnston (lead singer of Mango Groove): "When I was younger and caught up in my first great romance, I thought love was all about passion and torment, sleepless nights, agonizing jealousy, and lots of unhappiness.

"Over the years, I have started seeing it quite differently: Real love has an unselfish lightness to it; it's about really seeing the person you love as separate from yourself and wanting them to be the best and happiest they can possibly be, with or without you.

"I think I learned this from my husband, John, whom I was lucky enough to meet when I joined Mango Groove. We started out as colleagues and became friends, and then one day something else just happened. That was a long time ago, but I am increasingly aware of how lucky I am that he has such wisdom and kindness, and that he gives me all the space I need to realize my dreams."

Ashley Hayden (actress/television presenter): "I always think that love is a verb, not a noun. It's not something you say, it's something you do."

Theuns Jordaan (singer/songwriter): "Liking someone, or loving their strengths and positive attributes, comes naturally and easily. Love is the acceptance and understanding of someone's weaknesses and shortcomings; the willingness to serve someone without wanting anything in return. It's not a transaction; it's about how much you can love those imperfections."

Nataniël (singer/songwriter/entertainer): "Love is the condition in which I am eventually able to forget about myself because someone else is more important. Love is the cessation of judgment or doubt in which someone else's safety, survival, and happiness become my unconditional priority. As an adult, it is (aside from all the tears and drama) much more important, healthier, and more satisfying to love than to be loved. You can only say that you have truly lived when you have really loved."

Loyiso Bala (singer/songwriter): "Love is like a curtain rail for me. The most important things in my life—hope, peace, and joy—hang on it. As long as I am in the presence of love, I will always be safe and protected."

Leon Schuster (comedian/filmmaker): "Love is the ultimate 'kick in the gut,' equal to the feeling you get when you see the Creator's handiwork from space for the first time."

Cindy Nell (Miss South Africa/model): "For me, love is patience; thinking before you speak. Love is listening and sometimes not giving your opinion. Love is respecting the things that are important to someone even if they're meaningless to you. Love is building up and never breaking down. Love is seeing the beauty and cultivating it; there's always beauty to see."

Steve Hofmeyr (actor/singer/songwriter/author): "Never have so many indefinable enormities been tied together in so few letters: love."

Margit Meyer-Rödenbeck/"Dowwe Dolla" (actress/comedian): "Love is *choosing* to focus on someone's strengths instead of their weaknesses."

Nicholis Louw (singer/songwriter): "My head almost exploded now; my thoughts on love are so complex that I simply can't sum them up. Love is the foundation for the survival of humanity, a gift from God. God *is* love; we are nothing without God. We are nothing without love."

Jennifer Jones (singer): "Love is the only powerful force that overcomes all that is not God."

Glenys Lynne (lead singer of Four Jacks and a Jill): "I only really experienced 'being able to love' for the first time when I gave my life to Jesus Christ and invited Him to come and live in my heart in 1979.

"Within minutes of doing that, I had a new perspective on love. Love understands why others are not the way you expect or want them to be. I believe a mother's love for her children is probably the closest to God's love because it is unselfish and mostly unconditional. She loves her children no matter what they do and will shield them with her own body and her whole being. Love can teach us to control our tongues. Women find it easier to love than men do, but they are required to respect men (particularly their husbands). It also seems that men find it easier to respect their wives than to love them. Love is what makes us honor our elders and stops us from hurting others in anger. It loves truth and always believes the best of everyone. Being the most excellent way to live and the hardest, it is my highest aim. Love is not soft—it is the strongest force there is. Love is stronger in action than it is in words. It doesn't ask for or expect any returns."

Dr. Michael Mol (producer/presenter): "For me, love is perfectly described in Corinthians 13:4–8: 'Love is patient, love is kind … Love never fails.' Couldn't do better than that!"

Louise Carver (singer/songwriter): "There are lyrics in one of my songs that go: 'Sometimes love's not enough, he would leave regardless.' Although that sounds cynical, I truly believe that you need much more than just 'that feeling' for love to go the distance. A shared value system and a desire to stay when the going gets tough are just two of the qualities that two people need for their relationship to be more than just a season or a reason."

Heinz Winkler (*Idols* winner/singer/songwriter): "I believe love was created by God, and He gives us the best example of how to actualize it by practicing unconditional, unselfish, and service-oriented sacrifice—to those who are closest to you as well as to strangers. I also believe that the extent to which one can fully love is directly proportional to his or her spiritual health. The more certain of yourself you are, the less emotional baggage you carry, and the more you will be able to love. Getting there is a journey and it isn't easy, but that's what I strive for because I know it's the best way to live."

Judith Sephuma (singer/songwriter): "Love is contentment, confidence, and, more than anything, self-worth. Giving kindness is love, being patient with others is love. Most of all, loving unconditionally without expecting anything back is amazing for me."

Dozi (singer/songwriter): "Love is the way Jesus loves us."

Riana Nel (singer/songwriter): "When I don't fear punishment anymore, then I am truly allowing myself to be loved."

Lira (singer/songwriter): "Love heals, fear brings dis-ease. Love opens up and fear closes in. Love brings us closer while fear tears us apart. Love sets us free while fear keeps us frozen. Love breeds the courage to conquer fear.

"I believe that love is the very essence of who we are … we express it through action; love is a *verb!* Mostly, it is what connects all of us, making us treat each other with understanding, compassion, kindness, and gentleness."

Nádine (singer): "Love is the only irrational emotion that can both break and build. It understands no logic or reason; it can bring tears and happiness in the same moment. Love eludes every word that describes it, but it is found everywhere. Love is endless."

Brümilda van Rensburg (actress): "Love is God's all-encompassing love for us—'I have called you by name; you are mine' (Isa 43:1, NLT)."

Lize Beekman (singer/songwriter): "Love is everything we can hope to live, to know, and to experience in a lifetime, summed up into a single word."

Rina Hugo (singer): "God is love. If you let Him into your life, love will flow into every facet of your life. Love softens everything. Love is unconditional."

Sophie Ndaba (actress): "When someone has love, they possess inner peace; it's easy to have faith when you have love. When I love, I am happy, so to me, love is the key to all that is good. It sustains the worst relationships and turns pain to peace. If you don't have love, you have no life. Love is my lifeline!"

Elizma Theron (singer): "Love is … love. There isn't a stronger word to describe the feeling. The word 'love' includes many smaller meanings … but those are the things that make it what it is and give it its power; all those meanings are included when someone tells you they love you. Love is not just about loving the parts of someone that are easy to love … it's almost more about loving their faults and the things that irritate you about them."

Chris Chameleon (singer/songwriter/actor): "I have no idea what love is. The greatest poets, artists, and composers have been trying to express it over millennia, and it's due to their failure that we still create beautiful failures in our attempts to define it."

Vicky Sampson (singer): "Love … I believe that it truly starts from within, and that getting to know yourself really well is the key to real love.

"I feel real love for myself at last and that is why I am able to love others more willingly, with absolute honesty, and with no expectations. The road has been long and tough, but I have asked myself all the relevant questions, been brutally honest with my answers, and now that I am able to love myself better, I am not so needy of external love.

"It works for me and obviously it goes deeper than that, but this is how I will try to live my life from now on. There is no longer that constant desire to be liked or needed by all and sundry … and it makes life so much simpler. I try to love everyone who crosses my path, not because I have any expectations, but because I believe that this is God's plan for us."

Mara Louw (singer/*Idols* judge): "Great is the power of might and mind, but only love can make us kind, and all we are or hope to be is empty pride and vanity. If love is not part of all, the greatest man is very small. Yes, love is the language every heart speaks, and love is the answer to all that man seeks."

Derrich Gardner (television and radio presenter): "Love is when you say what you think, and not say what you think you should say."

Carike Keuzenkamp (singer): "To love someone unconditionally, that's true love for me."

Sorina Erasmus/"Witbank Flooze" (actress/singer): "God is love. You don't get more than that, and less than that is not honest, eternal love. That's the fundamental component of any type of love, relationship, or meaning of the simplicity of love."

Kurt Darren (singer/songwriter/television presenter): "I can't negotiate about love; it's a necessity for me, something that I have to begin and end my day with."

Burgerd Botha (singer): "True love is sharing every aspect of your life with someone, unselfishly and unconditionally."

André Venter (singer): "For me, love is definitely one of the most important components of society! I believe that love always wins no matter what the circumstances.

"I wish we could all radiate love like children do. I am amazed by my boys; they don't care what I do, even if I sometimes behave badly toward them, they just have an ability to radiate love for me and love me more. The miracle of love is that you can swallow your pride and forgive if someone has wronged you. Loving your partner unconditionally is what love means for me personally."

Louis Loock (singer): "Love is a moment that stretches between two people until one of them is no longer there. The other will continue to believe in it until the day it becomes possible to describe God's love in Heaven."

Adam Barnard (singer): "Love is when someone can see the best and worst of the beloved and still be inspired by it; when you are spellbound by every moment and every movement that person makes."

Sonja Herholdt (singer/actress): "Love is what love does."

Jay (singer): "Love is so much bigger than we can imagine. We're not capable of tainting love—only of accepting it, of choosing to love or not to love."

Gloria Bosman (singer): "Love is a beautiful phenomenon that we try to define with our minds, but it was never meant to be understood by the brain; it is pure!"

Francois Henning/"Snotkop" (singer): "I think what the world has forgotten is that love can solve hunger, aggression, and any war. Even the anger and sadness in your own heart can be soothed by self-love. Love is power, and if you love yourself, everyone around you will also experience love. Love heals."

Ray Dylan (singer): "What is love? That's probably one of the most difficult questions faced by mankind.

"There are different kinds of love, in my opinion. For instance, the love you have for your mother is not the same as your love for your partner.

"But the recipe for true love is: trust, respect, patience, and forgiveness. If you mix these four components with desire and passion, you will end up with a bond that is hard to break. That bond is true love."

Patricia Lewis (actress/television presenter/singer): "Love is all encompassing, deliciously painful, agonizingly pure, disruptively calming, magnificently mad, insanely logical, sobering but intoxicating, chaotically tranquil, vulnerably strong, excruciatingly satisfying; pure, raw, undiluted emotion; ultimately amazingly beautiful, beautiful, beautiful …"

OUR CHILDREN

Aneldre (11): "For me, love is a wonderful thing. When I wake up in the morning, my cat comes and 'head bumps' me, and when I sit up, I see the flowers and trees in the garden and the blue sky. In the afternoons at the beach, I look up and see birds flying in the blue, cloudless sky, and as I walk I feel the sand between my toes and the cold water splashing my feet. When I look around me, I see dogs running around and trees blowing in the wind. When I go home, my parents are there, and we go for walks together. I love playing with my cats and dog, and I give them attention by stroking their heads. All of this is God's creation: the blue sky, the dark night, plants, and animals. When I see them, I feel the love that God felt when He created them. Love is a warm, content feeling that is in everything around you. It's very valuable, and a person should always cherish it. My *Ouma* and *Oupa* have been married for 56 years, and when my *Oupa* looks at my *Ouma*, his eyes twinkle. Love is: carrying on, enduring, and having courage."

Merisa (8): "Love has to be everywhere, because if there is no love, the world is sometimes very hard. You must have love in your heart. You just have to believe, and then you will have love, and everyone will like you and love you. Is it not so that we are all very special?"

Heinrich (13): "Love is that knot you feel in your stomach when you're around that person. Or that sudden urge to hug your cat or dog. For a boy, his muscles pull tight, he smiles, and starts screaming in his head."

Ruan (13): "Love doesn't only have one meaning—yes, that's right, love has two meanings. Your parents love you, and you are in love with your neighbor's daughter. I think love is cool because without it there wouldn't be anything to distract you in math class."

Dirk (8): "I love myself because I have got a good little heart. I like myself because I am clever and I want to make all my mother's dreams come true. My father is good to me because if I play badly he tells me it was good, but he knew it was bad. It's a wonderful life. One of the most important things is God."

Gabriel (4): "Love is when I want to kiss my mommy."

Francois (11): "Love is ... I don't know. You can't describe it—well, I can't. But what I do know is that love isn't when you see a girl in a tight short skirt. That's just looking for attention."

Kaylynne (9): "Love for me means angels and butterflies are dancing in my heart. Love is also God, and God also loves fish. One fish died because he was sick. His name is Blue Eyes, but he is with God."

Vincent (13): "Every time I look into her eyes I feel like I'm going to faint. Then I tell myself, 'You can do it, you can talk to her.' Then I get to her and my legs feel like jelly and I stutter. For me, love is the closest thing to magic."

Lilliano (13): "Do you believe in love? Well, I definitely don't; well, not now. In the morning when my dad gets up, he asks my mom, 'Have you made my coffee yet?' Then my mom gets up still half asleep, makes him breakfast, gives it to him, and goes back to sleep. My dad doesn't even say, 'Thank you, my darling.' Then he climbs into his car and goes to work. That's why I don't want to believe in love. Men, and sometimes women, too, have ups and downs."

Marco (13): "Love is stable and doesn't fall over easily."

Philip (10): "Love feels like a shock. And you know the person is the one. But if the person is a bully or doesn't believe in Jesus, it's the wrong one."

Wian (8): "Love can be lots of colors, for example, yellow, blue, red, and pink. Love can sound like anything, for example, trees, songs, and waterfalls."

Jeandre (13): "If you have love, you are always happy and you smile the whole time. Love can also hurt, or lead to death."

Melanie (12): "Love is lovely, comfortable, incredible, emotional, and to your benefit. There are three different kinds of love: (1) You love your family (not your brother so much); (2) You love your dog or cat (I am a fan of both); (3) The most incredible love is the love that gives you butterflies in your stomach, that makes you blush like a tomato. That's the love that you have for that special girl or boy. The one that you dream about at night, the one that you just want to grab and kiss. That's the greatest love, so if I were you, I would hold on to that love."

Nichol (12): "Love isn't something you want to lose. Love is something that you shouldn't take too far; you must know what you're doing!"

Johan (12): "Think about it: Love is like proteins, carbohydrates, fats, vitamins, and minerals. If you don't eat them you become sick; if you eat them you're healthy and you can play nicely instead of going to the hospital."

Tristan (10): "Love is a beautiful thing in the air where everyone breathes. Love is so beautiful that no one can tell you how it feels; [you] only [know] if you have felt it. As soft as the softest teddy in the world, but softer."

Wehan (12): "Love hurts, but it's wonderful for someone who is in love with someone. If our world didn't have love, we wouldn't exist. I am so glad that I'm not in love, because girls easily break your heart."

Tessa (12): "Love is like boys: messy and unpredictable. Love is always in the right place. The only problem is that you are not always in that place. Love is like chocolate: It can be sweet or bitter. In the end, love is like a cell phone. It is always with you and the most important thing in your life."

Antoni (12): "Love is that transparent thing we all have somewhere in our hearts. For some it is just a little bit more difficult to see than others."

Caila (12): "Many people are sad, alone, weepy, and cross, with many other feelings as well. Many times these people just need a bit of love. It is almost like drinking medicine when you are very sick. Love everyone, because if you were that person, you would feel the same."

Nardus (13): "Love is the feeling you get when you see that person who just looks so darn pretty, even if that person is dog ugly to other people. If you love someone, you will make sacrifice after sacrifice for her—giving her your homework which she didn't do, taking the blame for her. And to say thank you, she will give you a kiss."

Arinda (17): "Love knows when to chatter and when to listen. Love's antics make you giggle. Love comforts a sore heart. 'Mom' is another word for love."

Taylor (12): "Love is a wonderful thing because it makes you forget all the bad things that have happened."

OUR SENIOR MEMBERS

Pieter (90): "To love abundantly is to live abundantly. Without the touch of love, the human heart aches and the soul withers. That touch can also act as a creative influence. When we see beautiful works, we acknowledge that touch as the magical element that turns something ordinary into something marvelous. A child who grows up feeling loved will have a gentle heart. Love demands understanding and compromise. A wise man once said, 'Love is nature's second sun, causing a spring of virtues where he shines.'"

Myna (76): "As a flower needs the sun to become a flower, we need love to become human."

Charlotte (87):

Let love shine through your eyes today
As you greet a special friend
It may not be romantic love
But a love that has no end

Love can be shared in many ways

By giving a friendly smile
It could make a lonely one
Forget his trouble for a while

Love can break down barriers
And make a friendship last
It helps us to forget our sorrows

And mistakes made in the past

Love is a blessing from our God
This we surely know
As we share this love with others
Much more in our hearts will grow

Emsie (89): "Life has taught me that mutual respect, loyalty, and communication are the foundation of love. To be able to tell your loved one that you are still discovering talents that you never knew were there after years of togetherness—that makes your heart beat faster with loving gratitude for the fact that he is your husband."

Helena (80): "Love means that you will also walk the second mile together."

Lida (82): "Love is the most precious gift one can ever receive. If you receive it, treasure it."

Marina (60):
No day is too dark
And no burden too great
That God in His love cannot penetrate

The love you give to others
Is returned to you by the Lord
And the love of God is your soul's rich reward
God truly loves you come what may
He will lead you and protect you
Every step along life's way

Nancy (81): "Love is the cement that bonds and the oil that keeps the friction out of life."

Sandra (69): "Love is the first time my baby grandson smiled at me. It was heart-stopping."

Lucy (86): "Love is being sensitive to the needs of others and always being ready to lend a helping hand. With love in our hearts, we are always willing to walk the second mile with someone close, depending on who they are. Love understands; true friends and family will love you because they understand. Love forgives and forgets; those who love you will never hold the past against you. Love sometimes arrives suddenly through the back door that you unwittingly left open."

Pam (68): "For the lonely, love is tender words and kindness from a nurse."

Tienkie (75): "For me, love is a little blue-feathered bird. He usually sits on my shoulder and asks, 'Give me some bread please?' Then I'll butter some bread and we'll nibble on it together while he kisses my cheek or asks, 'Give us a kiss?' As soon as he's had enough, he says, 'I love you very much, my little darling.' There is so much love in his little bird heart, and he asks for so little in return—just my love."

Jeanette (67): "Love is the surprise you feel when your husband, who doesn't talk easily, suddenly says a full sentence."

Koekie (80): "In order to really love, you have to live close to God, because God is love. We are only capable of true love—even for husbands, children, or family—through Him. For me, love is also caring, especially here, where so many of us live together and you see the heartache and pain. Just a little visit made with love is such a beautiful gesture."

Edna (82): "Love is like a beautiful song, sung by two hearts in harmony beating as one. Love is a precious gift from God, and when you find it, hold on to it; never let it go. It brings happiness and fulfillment and is trusting and sincere. It brings out the best in everyone and has a ripple effect—the more you give, the more you get."

Salie (80): "God is love and we express that love by what we offer one another. Even though we try, we often fall short and fail to shine.

"A mother makes a huge sacrifice when she carries her baby in her body for nine months, doing everything she can to make the little one's life beautiful and good.

"Before he can even think or speak, a baby offers little hands that grasp and little eyes that look up at the mother compassionately as he receives the milk that nourishes him. It is important to remember that no words are uttered here. Hugs from Mom and Dad make his eyes shine and hidings bring tears. When he carries that special girl's suitcase for her, neither of them speak much. The effort she puts into looking beautiful for her matric [high school graduation] farewell and the car he finds to take her there safely are milestones, and we call them love; perhaps only puppy love, but still. When he places a ring on a special lady's finger, he pays a high price; perhaps too high for him, but hopefully it will only need to be done once.

Looking beautiful just for him on that special day costs her blood, sweat, tears, and sacrifice, but she will never think of it that way. And his hair might still be a mess, but he makes the effort to dress neatly for her, without even thinking about it. Their first home, later the first house they own, and eventually the dream house exactly as she described it. Even when times are dark and there are misunderstandings, a bunch of flowers is worth more than any number of words. When children come to repeat the cycle, the preparations he makes and the tokens he brings are worth more than the loveliest words. His presence in the maternity ward is a huge sacrifice. And when their sun goes down and they sit holding hands in the garden at the André van der Walt Old Age Home, that togetherness is worth more than any beautiful words. Yes, sometimes words are valuable, but I believe it's the things we do that truly demonstrate real love. Even toward our nearest and dearest, our love is confirmed by what we do and not by what we say."

Johanna (84): "Love comes to you with a single rosebud in a vase—'Are you happy here with us?'"

Rina (86): "The path of love is not always the easiest. Getting your child to make his bed when you and he both know that you can do it better and faster is love; saying 'hang your clothes in the cupboard, not on the chair' is love. Making a rule that he has to leave the bathroom in the same state he found it in (dirty clothes in the laundry bin, not on the floor); expecting homework to be done regularly and conscientiously of his own volition (no, your mother won't write the essay for you); telling him that rules and routine are necessary (not only to make his family life tolerable, but also for his own sake and the sake of the people around him when he takes on the big wide world).

"Yes, a child fulfills these requirements reluctantly; after all, the mother is 'just so old-fashioned.'

"Yet, when he's all grown up, he may realize that his mother enforced all those rules with a bleeding heart, and that underneath all of it lay a burning, loving desire to bring out the best in him."

Anetta (89): "Love overcomes the strongest storm and clears the darkest night."

Mercia (76): "Faith climbs the stairs that love made and looks through the window opened by hope."

Corrie (85): "Fullness of life doesn't lie in enormous wealth, approval, or the success of fame, but in knowing that someone cares about you. Spend time thinking of your loved ones; everyone yearns for genuine love."

Meintjie (81): "Where there is love there is no fear, because perfect love drives out all fear."

GENERAL

Andrew Thompson (my husband and the most important person in my life): "I don't know ... I'm waiting for your book to find out what love is."

Hanna Kok (my life coach, from her book *Make a Life*): "Unconditional love should not be confused with romantic love. Unconditional love is fearless and completely trusting. It is fearless, because we are not afraid to give too much, not afraid that others will not love us, not afraid of getting hurt or of not having enough. We are not afraid of life. We are completely trusting, not necessarily toward our life partners, but toward life and our Creator. We know that we are loved by ourselves and by our Creator. Love from anyone else is a bonus. We know that everything we give is given to the Creator and we cannot out-give God. We trust life.

"With romantic love, our main source of love and support is external. It comes from somebody outside of us. With unconditional love, our primary source of love and support lies within us. This enables us to be fearless and completely trusting."

Helen Keller: "Love is like a beautiful flower which I may not touch, but whose fragrance makes the garden a place of delight just the same."

Mother Teresa: "Love is a fruit in season at all times, and within reach of every hand. The success of love is in the loving—it is not in the result of loving."

Graham Cooke (international speaker/author): "Love is not about opening yourself up to another. It is choosing to be your real self no matter what occurs. Love is about how we love, not who loves us. 'I am what I love, not what loves me.' This has become one of the most powerful identity statements that I have ever made. It has produced a freedom that has revolutionized my relationships. Real love cannot be rejected, because it never seeks a return. Love is not an investment. It is the right thing to do. It is a part of our righteousness. That is, it is not just about doing the right thing, but more about being the right person. Be true to yourself and love others."

Biblical definition of love: "Love is patient, love is kind. It does not envy, it does not boast, it is not proud. It does not dishonor others, it is not self-seeking, it is not easily angered, it keeps no record of wrongs. Love does not delight in evil but rejoices with the truth. It always protects, always trusts, always hopes, always perseveres" (1 Cor 13:4–7, NIV).

MY CONCLUSION

The head nurse at a clinic once told me that when preschool-age children are asked to draw what they've seen after visiting the hospital, they all come out with different impressions. One child will draw a badge, another will draw a face mask, a third might draw an ambulance. Not one picture is the same.

So after all my research, I came to the conclusion that we each have a unique point of view; we think and experience things differently and one answer is not enough to satisfy all of us. In the end, love is what we choose it to be, how we choose to experience and express it.

I am often very inspired after watching movies; after watching *The Notebook,* I wrote a song called "How Beautiful Love Can Be." We might not be able to find an answer to what love is, but we do know how beautiful it can be.

HOW BEAUTIFUL LOVE CAN BE

Oh how beautiful love can be,
It erases the fear in me
It gives hope when there's none,
It's life begun
Oh how beautiful love can be,
It's the power God gave to me
It's the wisdom to see
And the patience to be
Give love the grace to belong,
Give it the space to carry on
Give love the strength to heal this world,

Give it a chance to show us our worth, to show us our worth,
To ease the pain, so we can start again

Oh how beautiful love can be,
It's forgiving, it's pure, it's free
It's to give without need,
To give indeed
Give love the grace to belong,
Give it the space to carry on
Give love the strength to heal this world,
Give it a chance to show us our worth, to show us our worth,
To ease the pain, so we can start again

ANGELS ALL AROUND US

There are angels all around us, reminding us that we are not alone and that we are loved unconditionally. Sadly, we often don't notice them. We are so busy trying to survive that we miss the special miracles they bring into our lives. I have received some poignant stories about how angels express unconditional love and reveal themselves in many shapes and forms. This reminded me that we only need to be aware to be part of the magic all around us. May these stories uplift your soul as they did mine.

Ilze Nel from Kimberley, South Africa: Friendship and Love
It was the end of October 2005 and we had just heard that we were all going to be retrenched [laid off]. It was a harsh blow, as my career was very important to me. I loved my job; I had made many friends there, and we even had a colony of feral cats that we took care of.

One of the queens in the colony was a prolific breeder. In October we noticed that she had kittens on the way again, and when she disappeared for two weeks, we knew that she was nursing. When she appeared again, she brought two black kittens with her, a male and a female. We noticed that there was something wrong with the male. His sister was much larger than he was and very protective over him, and we could see that his eyes were whitish gray. We kept tabs on them, but when a cold spell struck, I decided to take the little one to the vet, either to have him put out of his misery or to adopt him.

The vet confirmed that his sight was very limited, but insisted that one did not put blind cats down; after all, we don't put blind people down … what was I to do? He would never have survived as a feral, so I adopted him and named him Snipper. Snipper went everywhere with me. During my last two months of employment, I took him to work with me in a little basket every day so that I could feed him bottled milk and, later, wet cat food from a spoon.

When I was laid off, he became my constant companion. He slept in our bed with us, and if he needed the loo during the night, he would just ask to be let down and then hop into the basket next to the bed when he had finished. He never grew very big—he couldn't have weighed more than 3.5 pounds. He also never meowed; he just made "tick tick" noises when he was happy. He would sit on my lap when I worked on the PC or stretch out on my neck while I watched television. He coped well enough (as long as his food, water, and litter tray were always in the same place), and he still went everywhere with me. The people in town came to know me as the lady with the blind cat and would ask me where he was if they didn't see him.

During this time, I had obviously been applying for as many jobs as I could. In about September 2006, I finally found one and I was very happy about it.

Around the same time, Snipper started wetting me every time I picked him up. I took him to the vet to be neutered, thinking that this was the problem. He was, after all, a male cat and probably wanted to mark his territory, but after the neutering I noticed that the problem had become worse. He had also started walking on "tippy-toes" with his hind legs.

We went back to the vet, who did X-rays and found that Snipper couldn't empty his bladder naturally because he had brittle bones. Every time I picked him up, I put pressure on his bladder, making it possible for him to relieve himself, but he was in pain. The vet sent me home with him that night, but I knew that I had to make a decision; I couldn't leave my best friend in pain.

I went back and put him to sleep the next evening. I have never had to do anything so hard in all my life. The decision was easy; I wasn't going to make him live with his pain, but it was terrible to have to lose my friend. While I sat waiting for the vet, Snipper snuggled and cuddled into my neck for all he was worth. It was as if he wanted to comfort *me*. I cried so hard that the vet and all his staff, and eventually the patients started crying, too.

Soon afterward, I realized that Snipper had truly been an angel, sent by God to comfort me during my time alone with no job. He was always going to provide, but He knew that I needed something to take care of and love in the meantime. As soon as He did provide, his angel went home to heaven. He had been with me exactly as long as my joblessness lasted; one year with an angel! How lucky I have been to have received such unconditional love.

If nothing else, I know this: I will strive to be a better person, if only to see Snipper in heaven again—because no heaven will ever be heaven without my Snipper to welcome me.

Sister Claudette Musgrave from Johannesburg, South Africa: *Love Overcomes All*

As the midwife in a maternity ward, a lot of the experiences and situations that cross your path can really touch your heart.

One day I admitted a patient (let's call her Lisa) who was already in labor when she arrived. She had come to the hospital alone, and told me that this was her third baby. As I won her confidence over the course of her labor, she told me her story.

Her husband (Gert) had become involved in an argument (in Lisa's defense) that had come to blows. The man was admitted to the hospital and died of his injuries, and Gert was charged with assault and homicide and sentenced to five years in prison.

During his last year in prison, Lisa, who had waited for him faithfully until then, had a setback and fell pregnant. Her due date was right around the time that Gert was to be released, and she told me that she had decided it would be best for everyone if she gave her baby up for adoption so that she and Gert could start over. After giving birth to a beautiful baby daughter, she hadn't changed her mind.

Lisa and I did a lot of talking that afternoon, and I persuaded her not to sign the adoption papers. I was prepared to keep the "little pink foot" with us in the maternity ward until after Gert's release the following day, and I suggested to Lisa that she go and see Gert before deciding whether or not she wanted to tell him about the baby.

Two tense days passed during which we heard nothing, but the following day I saw Lisa walking down the passage, holding a man's hand tightly. She introduced him to me as Gert. She had told him everything, and he had said that there was no way that the baby should be given up for adoption. As far as he was concerned, it was their baby. He loved Lisa and understood the circumstances that had contributed to the pregnancy.

I couldn't stop myself. The tears just fell from my eyes. I will never forget the joy on the faces of both those parents as I quietly walked out of the maternity ward to give the three of them some time alone.

Later that afternoon, they came to fetch "little pink foot" after first going to fetch some clothing and blankets for her. I was very sad to see the little thing go, but at the same time, I was happy that her parents had found each other again. I knew that they were going to love each other as a family.

When Lisa and Gert visited with their three children a few months later, it was obvious to me that they had found their bliss.

Liz Hopkins from Yzerfontein, South Africa: Unexpected Love

What is unconditional love? It is not always the way a husband loves his wife, or vice versa; it's not even necessarily the love that a parent has for a child or the child for his parent. I experienced this very rare kind of love in the most unusual place. When my husband went looking for greener pastures, he left me with three very young children. Child support was a foreign concept for him, so life was stressful and challenging, but I found work at a factory as a secretary and gofer.

I had tremendous empathy for the women who worked there, and very soon understood that what I had perceived to be a tremendously hard life was really a walk in the park. I could not give enough praise and thanks for my cushy life when I compared it to the way these poor women were forced to live.

Most of them were sole breadwinners, supporting five and sometimes up to nine people. Their husbands would wait for them outside the factory on Friday afternoons and take the little bit of money they had earned that week for their weekend booze-ups.

One day, one of the elderly workers (who was riddled with arthritis and supporting a husband, son, daughter, and four grandchildren) came into my office. In her hands, she held a bunch of carrots and a bunch of beetroot, both of which she had grown in her own garden. Rather shyly, she said that she had heard I was bringing up three children on my own and asked me to accept her small gift. I was deeply touched. Wanting to do something for her in return, I offered to pay for them, telling her that I had planned to buy vegetables that very day. Not only had she saved me the trouble, but it was a bonus to receive fresh-out-of-the-ground goods. She refused to take my money. "God said we must live with open hands," she said. "What He puts into one hand, we should give with the other."

Some time after that I had to go for a relatively serious operation. I arrived at work on the morning before I was booked to go in, and there, on my desk, was a big present. I opened it to find a lovely vanity case and a pink dressing gown. It was an extraordinarily poignant gesture coming from women who had nothing.

The hospital was far away from where I lived, and my parents came to stay with my children. My friends let me know that they were very sorry but could not visit me; the 15 miles was too far for them to travel. Feeling rather sorry for myself, I resigned myself to a lonely stay. The night after my operation, I was lying in bed feeling very badly done by, when the door opened and in walked four of the women from the factory, carrying a small box of Black Magic chocolates and a little bowl of flowers! They had all clubbed together to hire a taxi.

I have never felt so loved or so touched. The tears just flowed. I was deeply touched by their completely unselfish gesture of love, and I will never forget that moment.

The day I went back to work, there was, once again, a present on my desk; this time, a bottle of Opium perfume.

I learned so much from those wonderfully generous and loving women:

Sometimes, you receive real, unconditional love where you least expect it. And the ones who can afford the least are the ones who give the most.

CHAPTER SEVEN

MUSIC, MY TEACHER

I have learned so much from being a musician and performing artist, and I am very grateful for this gift called music. Being able to sing and write songs is wonderfully fulfilling, and I am incredibly blessed. Through music I am able to express my emotions and feelings, escape reality at times, dream, inspire myself, motivate myself, encourage myself, and forgive myself. Music has taught me almost everything I know, and I am very thankful for this.

EGO

Sadly, I must confess that I wasn't always thankful. I remember resenting my talent when the teasing during high school became too much for me, and later in life I put a lot of pressure on myself to make something of my gift. I had extremely high expectations, and felt I owed it to myself and everyone I knew to make a success of my talent. In the early stages of my career, my burning ambition and desire for success consumed me night and day and turned me into a workaholic, and when I did achieve success, I still wasn't satisfied; I felt that my gift deserved more from me than I had already given.

According to Dr. Wayne Dyer, an expert on positive thinking, the ego will always try to convince us that our self-worth is measured by what we have, what we have achieved, and the approval we receive from others; and almost every problem in the world today stems from our need to accumulate more, our ambition to achieve more, and our need for approval. The ego can be ruthless; even more so

The ego can be ruthless; even more so when we do not realize that it is merely our false sense of self.

when we do not realize that it is merely our false sense of self. The true self needs nothing from this world; it knows that everything has already been done for us by the Creator of everything and that we are perfect and complete as we are.

I learned early on that life is not about what we accumulate—material wealth means nothing in the end—but I have struggled with ambition. I wanted to prove that I could achieve great success with my talent, and seeking approval has always been my biggest drawback.

There's nothing wrong with accumulating earthly possessions, being ambitious, or seeking approval, as long as we are spiritually motivated by unconditional love for ourselves and others, and not driven by the need to elevate the ego, receive something in return, or prove something.

Let me try to explain it this way: If I make music only to sell a lot of CDs, make lots of money, become famous, and please everyone, I might or might not end up being rich and famous, but I will most probably end up feeling unfulfilled.

The true self needs nothing from this world; it knows that everything has already been done for us by the Creator of everything and that we are perfect and complete as we are.

If I make music that comes from my heart and soul so that I can do what I love and uplift and inspire those with whom I share my music, I might or might not end up rich and famous, but I am guaranteed to be happy and fulfilled.

My ego sticks its ugly head out from time to time, and I often have to put it back in its place. If I am not aware of it, something will soon remind me. When I was chosen to become an ambassador for the "Be Namibian, Buy Namibian" campaign (for which the Namibian president is also an ambassador), I felt that it was a great honor to be able to represent the country of my birth, and I took time out of my busy schedule to fly there to help promote this campaign, even though I wasn't going to be compensated. I just assumed that they would be flying me business class (I am, after all, very important), and I was a bit offended when I found out I would be flying economy class. Sitting on the plane feeling unappreciated, I asked God if I was out of line, and immediately heard a voice in my head saying, "... and Jesus entered Jerusalem on a donkey." Well, that brought me back down to economy class in a hurry! We are all very important, but no one is more important than anyone else.

I have noticed that the most talented artists in the music industry are usually also the most humble. It's when we still feel that we have a lot to prove that our egos sometimes get the better of us. On the other hand, the opposite is also quite often the case, as beautifully illustrated in the television advertisement where an arrogant man says to the lady at an airport counter, "Excuse me, but do you know who I am?" She leans into the public address system and says, "Attention please, does anyone know this man? He doesn't seem to know who he is." When you feel offended by a person or a situation, you can be sure that it's your ego at work; it's good to be able to remind ourselves of that before someone else does it for us.

ATTITUDE

It was the beginning of December, and just like everybody else, I desperately needed a holiday. Even though the year had gone by quickly, I was exhausted. I was booked to sing some Christmas carols at a shopping center and, to be honest, I wasn't looking forward to it—partly because I only sing carols once a year and tend to forget the words, but mainly because I was just really tired.

As you can see, I had a negative attitude before I even arrived, so needless to say, things just went downhill from there. In my experience, a bad attitude always invites trouble. Before I knew it, things started to go horribly wrong.

We couldn't leave our equipment on stage because there were some dancers scheduled before us, so the stage had to be left clear. The dancers went over their time, and people started arriving, so we couldn't do a sound check, either. Then my sound engineer discovered that the sound system on site was too weak for the venue and that there wasn't enough space for him to stand in front of the stage where he normally does. It's virtually impossible to do sound from the side of a stage, but that was his only choice; all I could do was pray for a miracle in the sound department.

A bad attitude always invites trouble.

Soon after that, I found out that there were no dressing rooms—just a tent (occupied by dancers)—so I did my makeup on the grass behind the stage. As soon as the dancers left, I went into the tent to dress and discovered that there were no toilets, either. I always have to go before a show, so I ended up squatting in a corner of the tent. As I sat there, feeling sorry for myself and listening to the orchestra and four singers who were on just before me, I realized that they were playing almost all the carols I had prepared for the show.

I was still frantically trying to work out what to sing when it started drizzling, and the organizers came to tell me that they had asked the orchestra to wrap up immediately so that I would at least be able to go on before it started raining too hard. Did I mention that it was an outdoor venue? My poor sound engineer ran around like a headless chicken, trying to put all the gear back on stage and connect everything up as quickly as he could, but Santa was already there and the drizzle was scaring people off, so the venue started emptying out fast. By the time I went on, there was hardly anybody left to sing to.

Sitting on the side of the stage, my sound engineer couldn't hear what he had to do to stop the feedback from the tiny speakers. At one point he looked so help-less that I just started laughing. There were also some children running around and playing in the hay in front of the stage—they were having the time of their lives, so I couldn't get angry with them, but they were kicking up so much dust that I could hardly breathe, never mind sing.

We cannot change what has been done.

About ten people came closer to listen, so I sang my heart out for them. I was supposed to sing a half-and-half mix of carols and my own songs, but I was so rattled by all the prior events that I only sang about two carols and then focused on my own songs; they made me feel safer.

After the show I was really angry with myself because I knew that my negative attitude had made everything worse. I had also been unprofessional; I had allowed the whole situation to make me feel unsure of myself, and had given myself the security I needed by singing mostly my own songs instead of the Christmas carols the client had requested.

Unfortunately, we cannot change what has been done, but I wrote to the organizers and apologized sincerely because I believe we should take responsibility for our actions. Luckily for me, they were very understanding and even apologized to me as well.

There have also been times when my attitude has influenced situations posi-tively. When I was still doing background entertainment, I had to ask the ladies at the reception desk at the hotel where I was working to turn off the house music before I could start performing. They were always very busy and not very keen at all to help; I really had to nag them about it and often had to ask a few times. I knew I was just in their way and could see that they were becoming annoyed, so I decided to do something about the situation. The next time I performed there, I approached them with a huge smile and a friendly "How are

Having the right attitude in every situation is not always easy; sometimes it takes a lot of effort, but it always pays off in the end.

you guys?" I was still given the "treatment," but I decided to persist. By the third time, they greeted me as I approached, asked me how I was, and switched the music off without my even having to ask. Some time later, I did a corporate show at the same hotel, and there was a new girl doing background music in the lounge. I went to introduce myself, and we had coffee together. Not long into our conversation, she told me how hard it was for her to get the receptionist to switch off the house music. It was such an amazing feeling to be able to share my experience with her, knowing that what I had learned could help her, too.

I also discovered that my attitude could make a huge difference in the following situation. I used to withdraw and keep to myself if I sensed that I wasn't welcome or that people felt threatened by my presence. Sadly, this gave the impression that I was arrogant, unapproachable, or aloof.

I arrived at a birthday party once and could sense, as I walked in, that some of the guests felt nervous about having me there. Instead of withdrawing, I decided to hug everybody as I said a friendly hello. The tension dissipated immediately, and later, one of the guests admitted that she had enjoyed my company even though she had thought the party would be ruined when she had seen me walking in.

I believe my attitude will determine the outcome of every situation.

Having the right attitude in every situation is not always easy; sometimes it takes a lot of effort, but it always pays off in the end. If I have to compare the above incidents, the energy spent on being positive is far less tiring and the reward much more lucrative than energy spent on being negative. I make it my mission to put effort into my attitude since I believe it will determine the outcome of every situation I find myself in.

ENERGY

I am very aware of people's energy, especially when I am performing. When I am on stage, I feel the energy of my audience and of the musicians I am performing with. It takes very high energy levels to be able to pull off a successful performance, but thankfully this is not a problem for me; I always feel incredibly excited about performing, and just walking onto a stage gives me a boost, although that level of energy can be very difficult to maintain.

As the lead artist on stage, if I sense that the energy in the audience is low, I have to give a lot more to lift their energy to the point of enjoyment. If the energy of one of my band members is low, I have to give extra to make up for them. I cannot expect my audience to lift my energy levels—they've paid to come and see me ... to receive something special that I have promised to deliver, but I can only deliver it if my energy is electrifying.

To achieve this, I have to spend some time alone preparing myself to focus my energy before each performance. If you are a performer, or if you've had to give a speech in front of a room full of people, you probably have noticed that you become short of breath. This is a clear sign that your energy is all over the place. If your energy is unfocused, you might miss your target.

Here are a few Brain Gym techniques and a breathing exercise that I find very helpful for focusing.

1. First, I prepare myself well by running the order of the show in my mind, so that I know exactly what I am going to deliver.
2. I drink water to clear my mind.
3. I put one hand over my navel and use the thumb and middle finger of my other hand to gently rub the soft, hollow spots just under my collarbone. (Picture 1)
4. I cross my feet and hands, turn my palms to face each other, and then twist them inward toward my body. I just sit or stand in this position for a while, breathing slowly to calm myself. (Pictures 2–4)
5. While standing, I alternate between touching my right elbow to my left knee and then my left elbow to my right knee, breathing consciously while I do this. This exercise recharges me and reconnects the two halves of my brain, leaving me ready for action. (Pictures 5–6)

6.   I spend about five minutes focusing on one point while I breathe slowly. First I fill my lungs and then breathe out singing "ah" until my breath is finished. This calms me and focuses my energy.

7.   I gather energy by breathing in as I lift my hands up and breathing out as I bring them down.

8. I make a circle with my arms around my body, creating a "cocoon" of safe space around myself. Then I repeat the first up-and-down motion while breathing continuously.

9. Finally, I remind myself to have fun out there, because the audience will enjoy it so much more if I do.

Energy is a very important part of everything we do. This doesn't necessarily mean that we have to be loud or lively. Being a good listener requires energy; just being there for somebody also requires energy. In fact, everything worthwhile in life requires energy. People often ask me where my energy comes from, and I always joke and tell them that I am plugged into the main

If you love what you do and if you're passionate about life, life will provide you with the energy you need.

Source, God. If you love what you do and you're passionate about life, life will provide you with the energy you need. I know when I am not connected anymore because I can feel my energy levels dropping, and then I just do whatever it takes to engage with the main Source again.

TIMING

I often compose music with an unusual time signature. I can't explain why I feel the songs that way; it just feels natural to me—but I have learned that it makes my music a little bit more complicated to listen to, and I eventually had to teach myself to simplify my timing in order to make my songs more accessible.

The timing challenge in my music made me aware of the timing problems in my life. I would often pick the worst times to discuss things with people, and I needed to learn how to correct that. I still struggle with it at times, but awareness of a problem makes it easier to fix. It doesn't matter what you want to talk about or how right it is; if you've chosen the wrong time to say it, you won't achieve what you set out to do. People can't take

Instead of just focusing on what I wanted to say, I also had to focus on the person I wanted to say it to.

in what you're trying to say if they're otherwise occupied or if their state of mind isn't open to a discussion. There is an excellent chance that you'll be misunderstood or even that your message will simply fall on deaf ears. Bad timing can often just make a situation worse instead of resolving it.

The time signature of a song can change the feeling of the song totally. It's important to establish the mood you're trying to create before picking a time signature—and you also have to take your target market into consideration. I had to do the same thing in my approach to people. Instead of just focusing on what I wanted to say, I also had to focus on the person I wanted to say it to. When I did this, it became easy to pick up if the person was preoccupied or in a bad mood; I just had to be patient and wait for the perfect time to approach him or her.

My timing was all off on New Year's Day, 2011. I thought it would be a great idea to incorporate a spiritual exercise into our day instead of just partying into the New Year, so I took my pack of inspiration cards along with me and asked everyone if it would be okay if we did an exercise. Of course, they all said yes, but probably only because it was the polite thing to do. I first asked everyone to think about what they wanted to achieve spiritually this year and then we all picked a card. I was in my element ... I love doing this sort of thing! Everyone read their cards out loud, and I elaborated on what they had said just to make sure everyone understood. Halfway through the exercise, the men started disappearing (the children had already left after about the second card), and by the time we read the last card (mine), there were only two of us left. Everyone else had gone swimming or left to go and play on the grass ... you know, the sort of stuff you're supposed to be doing at that kind of party.

Everything happens at the right time and this cannot be changed no matter how hard we fight or resist it.

According to my husband, I also have a problem being on time. If he had his way, we would be at my performance venues the day before a show, while I prefer to arrive minutes before. His poor nerves can't handle it when I cut things so closely, but I can honestly say that none of my shows ever started without me! I have tried to explain why I like to slow things down, but it's an artist thing and someone from the corporate world might find it difficult to understand. I deliberately slow things down before a performance—I even try to slow my heart rate down, so that when I walk on stage and the adrenaline kicks in, I don't panic; I merely return to a normal state.

Everything happens at the right time; we can't change that no matter how hard we fight or resist. I used to get really impatient and wonder why things were happening so slowly for me, but looking back, I realize that everything happened at exactly the right time. The pace of things gave me space to grow and prepare for what was coming, and I have finally begun to understand, respect, and value time. I even wrote a song called "Only Time" in its honor.

Today I try to make time for people by taking my time with whatever I do. If I run into the shops for something small, it takes me a while because I chat with everyone (which is probably why my husband insists on going in himself). I am deeply thankful for the lessons time has taught me.

ONLY TIME

Time understands it all,
Has the final call, only time.
Knows what the future holds,
What the past has caused, only time.

It reveals and it heals, some will say it steals.
Can be cruel, has no rules,
Some will say it plays the fool.
But time understands it all,
Has the final call,
Only time.

Time never asks your name,
Or your claim to fame, it's all the same
It knows where we're going to,
It will see us through, only time.

It reveals and it heals, some will say it steals.
Can be cruel, has no rules,
Some will say it plays the fool.
But time understands it all,
Has the final call, only time.

Time understands it all,
Has the final call,
Only time.

BREATHING

Breathing is vital to life, but it's also the most important technique in singing. While I was training to become a singer, I really focused on perfecting my breathing techniques. I used to think my breathing was pretty solid, but I was presented with a huge challenge when I had to perform with Andrea Bocelli.

Whenever I am about to face a challenge or enter a new situation, I study, I research, I train, and I do everything in my power to prepare myself properly; that way I can avoid being caught off guard. One of the songs I had to sing with Andrea was partly written in Italian. I needed help with the pronunciation, but I also needed help with the last note in the song, so I went for singing lessons. Andrea is an amazing singer with unbelievable breath control, and when he sings this note, he holds it forever and ever … and then just a little bit longer … because he can.

I became a little nervous every time I had to sing that last note; I would take a deep breath, hold the note for as long as I could, and then push, forcing the last little bit of breath from my lungs to hold it a bit longer, but it was never enough. I would still hear Andrea's voice carrying on and on even though I was blue in the face.

Draw life in and don't push or force things. Allow life to carry you, relax, and have faith that it will take you where you need to go.

Then my teacher, Mattie le Clus, taught me something amazing. She told me to imagine drawing air in, instead of pushing out, while I was singing the note, and encouraged me to relax into it and allow it to carry me rather than try to carry it. I couldn't believe how well it worked. Immediately after applying this principle, I could hold the note much longer than I had been able to before. How often do we push and force things, only to end up short of what we desire? We need to draw things in, instead of pushing outward. We need to allow life to carry us, instead of trying to carry life.

When I went up on stage that night, my main goal was to allow the song to take me wherever it wanted to. I enjoyed every minute of it, and even though Andrea still held that last note longer than I could, I smiled in admiration, marveling at how much I had learned from the experience: Draw life in and don't push or force things. Allow life to carry you; relax and have faith that it will take you where you need to go.

COMMUNICATING AND CONNECTING

My mother is one of the best communicators I know. Wherever we went, my mom would make friends and chat up a storm. I always admired her confidence and genuine interest in people, and often wondered how she did it so naturally. Communicating has never been something that comes naturally to me; I have had to work very hard at it.

I always found it very difficult to engage in small talk; I just wanted to get to the point, especially in business. Later on I learned that small talk is vital because it helps to create a connection, and you can only communicate with someone effectively once you have connected with them.

You can only communicate with someone effectively once you have connected with them.

If you know how to connect with people, you will be able to make a success of whatever you do. There are thousands of performers out there, but it's the ones who know how to connect with their audiences who continue to play to full houses. Great connectors are the people who are most effective in business, and a teacher who can connect will be able to teach any student. My mom was an amazing teacher. Today I know that it's because she knew how to connect.

Connecting is not just vital in business; it's what life is all about. Life is so much more fulfilling if you can connect with people.

In his book *Everyone Communicates, Few Connect,*[1] the great communicator and author John C. Maxwell makes it easy for anyone to learn how to connect. According to him, connecting is not about "me." If I want to connect with others, I have to get over myself and change my focus from inward to outward.

It reminds me of that saying: "Okay, I've talked enough about me now ... so what do you have to say about me?"

It's easy to talk about what we know, what is going on in our lives, what we think, and what we've experienced, but talking about ourselves doesn't help us connect with others. Connecting takes effort. We have to take the time to discover what is going on in that person's life—what he or she is thinking and has experienced. The only

Connecting takes effort. We have to take the time to discover what is going on in that person's life— what he or she is thinking and has experienced.

way to do this is to ask questions and then listen with genuine interest. When we ask people questions, we discover what we have in common with them, and then having a conversation becomes much easier.

This principle works wonders in one-on-one situations and also in groups, but connecting with an audience is a little different. As a performer I can't very well stand on stage and listen to my audience—they have paid money to come and listen to me—but the principle of focusing outward still applies. My aim must be to give my audience something special; to share my heart and soul passionately, honestly, and positively. To make my audience feel what I am feeling, I need to be sincere and willing to give completely, without expecting anything in return.

> *To make my audience feel what I am feeling, I need to be sincere and willing to give completely, without expecting anything in return.*

I need to make my audiences feel comfortable and safe, but I can only do that if I feel comfortable and safe with myself. An audience becomes uncomfortable if they sense uncertainty. Walking onto a stage in front of thousands of people can be very daunting, and that makes it easy to lose your focus and—if you're unprepared—to make mistakes, so it is essential for me to be well prepared for performances.

It's also hard to be confident in front of an audience if you are not comfortable with yourself yet. Being comfortable with yourself comes from loving and accepting yourself over time. It took me around 39 years to achieve this, and I still lose confidence every now and then. In those times, I remind myself that we are all the same; we just want to be loved and accepted. It is my desire to communicate just that to my audience—that I love and accept them—and that is only possible when I love and accept myself.

> *It is my desire to communicate just that to my audience—that I love and accept them—and that is only possible when I love and accept myself.*

I have come a long way in communicating with my audiences. I used to be so shy that even saying thank you after a song was overwhelming for me, and having to express myself in two different languages was nerve-racking. I was fluent in both, but I never knew what to say. I also hadn't grasped English humor yet—something hilarious in Afrikaans doesn't always have the same impact in English.

Another valuable lesson I learned from John Maxwell's book is that positivity comes from believing in people. This is especially true on stage. I must have faith, not only in what I am offering, but also in my audience, and I remind myself of

I must have faith, not only in what I am offering, but also in my audience.

this all the time. It's hard to remain positive if you lose faith in your audience; if they pick up on this, your connection with them will be compromised.

Having faith that my audience will accept what I have to offer has been a big struggle for me. When people are very quiet during a performance, I have sometimes misinterpreted their silence, only to be surprised by the response after the performance when they purchase a lot of my CDs or tell me how much they enjoyed the show.

Finally, I need to connect with my music. When I sing what I believe in and what I am passionate about, my music will connect with others.

BREAK A LEG

I have no idea why people say "break a leg" before a performance; I don't think it ensures good luck. I have never broken a leg, but I did once break a shoe and had a very embarrassing fall on stage. Just before going on that day, I had commented to one of my band members that the stage was so uneven, I was probably going to break my neck, and as I walked back on for the encore, it almost happened. My shoe got stuck in the carpet, and I went flying through the air in front of a full house.

As I glanced down, I noticed that my toe was bleeding where the shoe (now broken) had cut into it. I had to continue barefoot, which was a total nightmare for me; I hate being barefoot. I don't even walk from my bed to the en-suite bathroom without putting shoes on … now I had to do a whole song on a dirty carpet with no shoes, a bleeding toe, and a bruised ego. I held back the tears, but when the curtain dropped, I sobbed. I was still licking my wounds and feeling very sorry for myself when one of my band members came to tell me that there were four young fans outside asking for "Nádine." That was funny enough to make me feel better immediately.

Nádine is another successful South African artist, and people often confuse the two of us. I did feel a bit sorry for her, because there were at least four people who thought she was the one who had taken the fall that night. I find it very entertaining when people confuse me with other celebrities; once a lady pulled me away to meet her husband just before I went on stage, and when we got to him, she proudly introduced me as Helene Bester (also a singer). I didn't want to let them down or embarrass them, so I just gave him a warm hug and even took a photo with them. I hope they weren't too disappointed when they found out I wasn't her. Maybe they never did.

I also once landed on my rear in front of a big group of people after a Skouspel performance at Sun City (a resort in the North West province). At this annual event, musicians perform for audiences of about 5,000 people for seven shows in a row. We were staying at the Sun City Vacation Club, and we took the girls for a swim after one of the shows. Everyone seemed to recognize me as I walked in—partly because most of them had just seen the show and partly because our triplets are a dead giveaway. Feeling self-conscious with everyone's eyes on me, I didn't feel brave enough to reveal myself in a swimsuit and decided just to wet my feet with the girls. As I walked into the shallow water with Tayden in my arms, my foot slipped and I landed flat on my back. Thankfully, the water softened my landing and I was able to hide my face behind Tayden, but sitting there, I thought, *You know what—I'm wet anyway, and letting everyone see me in my swimsuit can't be any worse than what just happened* ... so I took off my wet shorts and T-shirt and went swimming. In no time, all the children in the pool surrounded us, and started telling me how nice the show was and asking me if I knew any of the other celebrities personally. Not long after that, some of the mothers also gathered around us, and I couldn't help but wonder if my fall or perhaps my cellulite-y bum had given them the courage to join in. However, I was once again reminded not to be too hard on myself by thinking I should be perfect in every way.

I was once again reminded not to be too hard on myself by thinking I should be perfect in every way.

Not too long after this, I fell down a staircase at our house and tore a ligament in my left knee. I was storming down the stairs in a temper about having to look for something that someone had moved for the umpteenth time, when I missed a step and fell down another seven stairs before landing on all fours. The fall was so serious that I had to cancel a few performances, but it gave me a much-needed rest and also taught me a lesson: Never mix anger with stairs.

I had to walk down a runway with some models at a charity event once, and the fact that I wasn't singing made me very nervous. The well-known South African model Christina Storm gave me this advice: "Being a model is not brain surgery. Just walk, and when there is no more ramp, stop! Then turn around and walk straight back, and remember, it's when you think you're fabulous that you will fall."

TUNING

It's extremely painful for a musician to perform on an instrument that is out of tune—and not very pleasant on the audience's ears, either. I love playing on a grand piano, but we hardly ever find one that's in tune, so I use a Clavinova, which is an electronic keyboard with weighted keys. It sounds and feels just like a piano, except that it doesn't need to be tuned. The crew hates my Clavinova because it's really heavy, but I refuse to play on anything else.

In the same way that a musician needs a well-tuned instrument to be able to enjoy performing, we also need to be in tune to enjoy life.

In the same way that a musician needs a well-tuned instrument to be able to enjoy performing, we also need to be in tune to enjoy life.

Well-known motivational coach Anthony Robbins once made a comparison that I love. He explained that a piano needs to be tuned frequently at first so that the strings don't slip, but once the strings have adjusted to their new tension, the piano won't need to be tuned so often.[2] People are also like that. We feel all fired up after hearing a motivational talk or seeing an inspirational performance, but we soon return to our old way of thinking. That is why we need tuning quite often, especially if we have been stuck in negative thought patterns. When I started seeing a life coach, I went weekly; later on, once a month. Now I only go when I feel that I need to.

Every now and then I become a bit difficult or negative, and then my husband asks me if perhaps it's time to go and see Hanna again. Each of us knows what keeps us in tune; it's different for everybody. Spending time with positive people, reading uplifting books, and going for sessions with my life coach all help me stay in tune. Remember: Not only does life become unbearable for you when you're out of tune, but it's also unpleasant for the people around you.

We need tuning quite often, especially if we have been stuck in negative thought patterns.

TONE

I mentioned before that my voice was already well developed by the age of eight. I had a natural operatic tone, but this became a bit of a problem because I wanted to sing light music. Imagine a song like Tina Turner's "Simply the Best" sung with an operatic voice; well, that's how I sounded in the beginning. I realized it wasn't working when the owner of a pub we were playing at asked us to please let someone else in the band sing for a while.

During my first year of studying light music, I also trained in opera and soon realized that the two styles clashed. My light music teacher would often tell me I sounded too operatic, while my opera teacher felt I needed to spend more time on classical voice training. The classical training techniques were extremely valuable in developing my voice, but I eventually decided to focus on light music since that was where my passion lay. I spent a long time working on my tone to make it more acceptable for light music, and I got to know my voice very well during this process. I learned how to manipulate it to create the sound I liked by recording myself and listening to it. Your voice sounds very different over speakers, and it's important to listen to it before you embark on a singing career. It's very clear to me that some of the aspiring singers who enter competitions such as *American Idol* and South Africa's *Idols* have never heard their own voices in this way.

Every style of music requires a different tone, and different tones used in a single song can lend texture and color. To achieve this, you can "place" the note in your head or throat, or make it come from your stomach. "Placing" notes before you sing them also helps with pitch; first you hear the note in your mind and then you sing it.

It's not always what we say, but how we say it that determines how well it will be received.

Tone is vital in putting the right message and feel across, and this is something I have also learned in life. It's not always what we say, but how we say it that determines how well it will be received. Often my delivery would be too strong and powerful. I needed to think before I spoke and "place" the information before projecting it. By doing this I learned how to deliver my messages with the correct tone. The effect that the tone of someone's voice can have on people is amazing. You may have noticed that listening to someone speaking loudly in a high-pitched tone is often difficult, but everybody leans in to hear better when someone drops his or her tone and speaks softly.

Men find it hard to listen to high frequencies. I think that's very funny because most women raise their pitch when they are upset or excited. I have learned from experience that a high-pitched tone (and believe me, I can deliver a very high note) is not the way to put my message across to my husband, although it does sometimes help me rid myself of frustrations.

SIMPLICITY

One thing I do well is to listen to good advice from people who know what they're talking about. I have worked with many wonderful producers during my career, and quite early on, one of them told me that the verses in my songs seemed stronger than the choruses. The chorus of a song should be the strongest part of the song; that's where you're supposed to capture the song's essence.

I gave his critique a lot of thought and eventually realized what my mistake was: I would take the first idea that came to me (which is usually the best and freshest one) and use it as my first verse—the beginning of the song. That meant that I had to come up with a stronger idea for the chorus, which often complicated my songs. What I needed to do was to make my first idea into the chorus. I have found that having an advanced ear can sometimes make it harder to write simple, catchy tunes. The way I used to write songs was to come up with clever and very difficult phrases that challenged me, but were too complicated for the average ear. It's the simple, catchy tunes that usually become hits because they're easy to listen to.

I eventually figured this out for myself by comparing music to movies. Most of the time, I like to watch nice romantic comedies with happy endings, endings that I can almost predict, because I like to relax while watching movies. Every now and then I'll watch a drama or suspense that I really need to concentrate on if I want to follow the plot, but mostly I like to keep it light. This realization helped me to understand the public's general ear for music. There is a place for every style, but most people prefer something light and easy to listen to. They want to relax after a long day—and what better way than listening to a song they can sing along to?

I managed to achieve simplicity in "Who Painted the Moon?" but as I said before, I felt the song was too simple to include on my first album. Later, I had another "Aha!" moment when I saw some five-year-olds singing along to it: If people can sing along to a song, it becomes easier for them to make it their own. At the end of the day, they also want to express themselves.

As children, we sing along with our favorite pop idol with a hairbrush in our hands while we pretend to be stars. As teenagers, we scream to our favorite rock band as we express our longing for freedom. As adults, we lose ourselves in the promise of a love song, and when we're older, we revel in the memories that songs evoke in us as we softly hum along.

There's magic in simplicity— it provides us with the space to experience magic.

Life can be like a catchy hit song or a romantic comedy, but we often turn it into progressive jazz or a suspense thriller. I have decided to try to keep it simple. There's magic in simplicity—it provides us with the space to experience magic. They say that we have about 60,000 thoughts every day; it's my goal to take that down to 10,000 a day so that I have more space to experience magic in my life.

EXPECTATIONS

Sometimes when I need some spiritual inspiration, I go to a pack of cards based on Dr. Wayne Dyer's book *Inspiration* and draw one. A few nights ago I picked a card with the following message:

Expect the Best
Change your expectations for yourself: Expect the best, expect Divine guidance, expect your fortunes to change, expect a miracle. When you were *in-Spirit* prior to materializing, your aim was high and your expectations were Godlike. Reacquaint yourself with that vision.[3]

I have always been careful with expectations. Experience has taught me that high expectations lead to disappointment (especially when you expect things from others), so when I read this card for the first time, I thought, *I'm not so sure about this one.* Then I read it again and again, and suddenly it became clear to me: I had to ask myself what "Godlike" meant, and align my expectations with that. If my expectations involved enriching myself, elevating myself, or focusing on "me, myself, and I," I would end up feeling disappointed. Our expectations should be centered on God. If I have expectations as if I'm still "in-Spirit," I will not be disappointed. Instead I will experience the best: "Divine guidance."

My fortune will change and I will experience miracles.

I had many expectations for this book, but I didn't expect the peace I have received from writing it. We are currently pitching my music in the United States, and I receive daily reports. Most of them read like this: "She has a wonderful voice, but we currently don't have any demand for that style of music." My favorite was the one in which they referred to me as an "old gal" and suggested that my music might work on the soap opera *Days of Our Lives*. I received similar feedback ten years ago when I pitched my music locally, and it devastated me then; today I am smiling and enjoying it. What's changed? I know my worth now; I don't need anyone's approval to feel worthy. I can accept negative feedback thankfully and humbly because I am experiencing "Divine guidance" and expecting more miracles.

> *If I have expectations as if I'm still "in-Spirit," I will not be disappointed. Instead I will experience the best: "Divine guidance." My fortune will change and I will experience miracles.*

THE POWER OF MUSIC

> *It occurred to me by intuition, and music was the driving force behind that intuition. My discovery was the result of musical perception.*
>
> – ALBERT EINSTEIN

The cultural diversity of South Africa makes our music industry unique. All the different languages and cultures divide our market into smaller groups, each supporting traditional styles of music in its own language. This makes it very challenging for South African artists, although there are a few who have managed to grab everyone's attention, and I salute them!

Music is a language that everyone can understand; I believe it unites us. I experienced one of my happiest moments performing at the 2010 FIFA World Cup finals held in South Africa, where various African artists/performers sang a song that was written for the occasion. I wrote the lyrics for the

> *Music is a language that everyone can understand; I believe it unites us.*

solo lines that I had to sing in Afrikaans, other lines were written in other African languages, and we all sang the chorus together in English. I thought I was going to explode with joy as I sang on stage that night. The energy was electrifying as we all united and sang together.

Music has saved my life, time and again, and I have received hundreds of e-mails from people telling me similar stories.

Music is more powerful than we can ever imagine. My father, who was a colonel in the police force, told me how they were taught to use music to calm angry mobs, and the events that took place on April 1, 1989, proved to him how effective music could be. Approximately 20,000 people participated in a celebratory march toward Windhoek in celebration after a free and fair election was confirmed for Namibia. This was an unauthorized and illegal march, and usually these marches led to plundering and violence, so the police decided to put a stop to it under the supervision of UNTAG (United Nations Transition Assistance Group).

The atmosphere was very tense, and if any of the role players had made a mistake, things could easily have turned into a bloodbath that day. While negotiations were underway, they played classical music to the crowd over the public address system (my father seems to remember a Strauss waltz). As always, it had a very calming effect, which helped the police convince the mob to turn around and go home peacefully.

Today there are many successful therapies that use music and sound to help people. According to the American Music Therapy Association, the sensory and intellectual stimulation that music offers can help patients maintain quality of life. Music therapy is used to increase or maintain the level of physical, mental, and social/emotional functioning for the elderly in nursing homes. In schools, music is taught to strengthen communication skills and physical coordination skills. In general hospitals, music is used to alleviate pain in conjunction with anesthesia or

To hear the music, we only need to listen … not just with our ears, but with our entire being.

pain medication, elevate patients' moods, and counteract depression. In psychiatric facilities, music therapy facilitates exploration of personal feelings, positive changes in mood, and conflict resolution leading to stronger family and peer relationships.[4]

Music has saved my life, time and again, and I have received hundreds of e-mails from people telling me similar stories. We often think of music as mere entertainment, but it is so much more. It can profoundly affect the way we understand ourselves and interact with the world around us. Spiritually, music creates a direct connection to God, a doorway through which we can experience, feel, and hear Him. People knew and experienced this thousands of years ago, and we are slowly starting to remember it again.

SILENCE

To hear the music, we only need to listen … not just with our ears, but with our entire being. To feel and understand the music, we need to become one with it; part of it. We need to become silent, quiet our minds, open our hearts, be still, and allow it to take us there, to where we can hear God.

FINALLY

Before I started writing this book, I asked myself these questions:

1. Why are you writing a book?
    Because I think everybody should write a book, or even just keep a diary. We learn much more, much faster, when we write things down.
2. What qualifies you to write a book?
    I have no qualifications on paper, but I think what qualifies me is that I am alive, I love, and it is my desire to share love.
3. Do you think this book will sell?
    It doesn't matter whether the book sells or not; what matters is that I wrote it.
4. What will you get out of this?
    This book will be my teacher, a reminder of the things that I will most probably forget as soon as life happens.
5. Who do you think might read this book?
    My mom.
6. What do you think love is?
    Love is us expressing ourselves unconditionally.
7. What is the purpose of this book?
    Me expressing my love.

What is the purpose of my life? Why am I here? Am I doing what I am supposed to be doing, and if not, how will I know what it is?

These are questions I am sure we all battle with from time to time; some of us all the time. I go through periods where I am absolutely sure of what my life purpose is and times when I question everything. We all want to make a difference. We all want our lives to have meaning.

Some will remember us for what we've achieved, but most will remember us for how we made them feel.

I was very moved by the service at a funeral that I attended not so long ago. The minister gently reminded us that we would all be lying in caskets one day, and then it would not matter how well we had done our jobs, how famous we were, or how rich we had become because we wouldn't be taking any of our earthly possessions with us. He asked us if we could remember the names of the last five presidents or if we knew who had invented electricity ... something along those lines. I didn't know the answers to his questions (but then again, my general knowledge has never been very good)—the point is that we all come and go. Some of us will do great things; others will just live ordinary lives. Some will remember us for what we've achieved, but most will remember us for how we made them feel.

There were a lot of people at that funeral, but it wasn't because the deceased had been rich or famous; she was just a very caring, loving, and giving individual, and people had loved her for that. People would remember her for that.

It made me think about my life and how I make people feel. I wondered if there would be people at my funeral (not that it will matter to me—I won't be here anymore), but perhaps asking these questions while I am still alive might help me to live with more purpose.

In business I have learned that knowing what end result I desire is the only way to achieve my goals. In life, as in business, if we do not know what our desired end result is, we end up wandering around aimlessly, hoping and praying that we are living a life that is worth living.

In life, as in business, if we do not know what our desired end result is, we end up wandering around aimlessly, hoping and praying that we are living a life that is worth living.

I often ask people what they think their life purpose is, and most tell me they wish they knew. We often think of the things we do every day as our life purpose—our jobs, raising our children, taking care of our families and ourselves—but surely life is more than just surviving and protecting ourselves and those close to us.

I think the purpose of life is to remember who we are in everything we do and experience, and to enjoy every moment—it's that simple. At the same time, it's not simple at all; remembering something you've forgotten takes time and effort, and there must be a willingness to remember.

Often we have to surrender what we think we know before we can remember.

Quite often we have to surrender what we think we know before we can remember.

We are all one, part of God's wonderful creation, spiritual beings sharing a physical experience. We are like a beautiful melody in which each of us represents a single note. If one note is missing or out of tune, the melody is no longer the same. When we feel low or negative, it affects everything and everyone around us. Therefore we need to take responsibility for each other as well as ourselves. We all determine how the melody will sound in the end. To perform our part in this exquisite song, we need to be compassionate, to care for each other and have empathy for each other. We are all responsible for the way the world is today—each and every one of us.

Are we, then, responsible for the things thieves, rapists, and murderers do? We might not be responsible directly, but I believe that indirectly we are. As the saying goes, "If you're not part of the solution, you're part of the problem!"

Perhaps we've desensitized ourselves to avoid taking responsibility for each other. We tell ourselves life is easier that way … but is it easier? I find it very difficult to live a carefree life knowing that there are desperate, angry people out there who will go to extreme measures, like killing, for a small amount of money—just to survive.

We are like a beautiful melody in which each of us represents a single note.

It is also possible that we have stopped caring because of greed; the fear that there might not be enough for us … enough food, enough land, enough money, enough power … the list goes on and on. We've created an uncaring world based on lies that stem from fear. I wrote "It's So Absurd" about 15 years ago, trying to capture the absurdity of our uncaring world.

IT'S SO ABSURD

When I see you, lying there,
I want to help you, need to care,
I want to take your hand
And make you walk away with me

But I'm not there,
Never would be,
I'm not strong enough to save you,
Strong enough to wipe your tears away and make you smile

It's so absurd, are we all blind?
Oh can't we change this world of ours?
How can you turn your back and walk the other way,
When someone's begging you to stay,
How can we not see them die?

When you told me,
I didn't listen,
Couldn't hear you,
Didn't see you dying
Hear you crying,
See you reaching out for me

So they carried on destroying
Every inch of life inside you,
Every breath and every dream
And every sound you've heard

It's so absurd, are we all blind?
Oh can't we change this world of ours?
How can you turn your back and walk the other way,
When someone's begging you to stay,
How can we not see them die?

All is gone, nothing's left, just memories,
The knowledge of what happened,
Of what could have been,
The fact there once was life,
Still we go on...

After writing this song, I often wondered how we could fix things, heal the world, and make it a better place. I felt hopeless not knowing what to do. When the news on my television set became too much to handle, I would just change the channel, and I felt awful about that. Thankfully the answer came to me with time, and I have realized that I do have the power to do something.

I can love. There's nothing more powerful than love! It starts within each one of us and circles out, but we have to love ourselves first. By merely thinking of this world and everything in it with love, I already make a positive contribution.

Even thinking of this world and everything in it with love, I already make a positive contribution.

We cannot love or care for anyone else if we do not love and care for ourselves first. Caring can be very difficult. It's sometimes so difficult that most of us just give up without even trying. Some of us will find any excuse to avoid it. Some will even end their own lives just so they don't have to care anymore. Ironically, the more we avoid caring, the more difficult and complicated we make our own lives.

I have avoided caring for myself for most of my life, and only when I became aware of this did I realize how important it is to face this challenge. Caring starts with understanding ourselves. We need to understand why we do things the way we do, why we react the way we do, why we make the choices we do, and why we think the way we do.

Once we understand ourselves better, the next step is to accept the things we can't change and work positively on the things we can. When we've managed to achieve that, we can work toward loving ourselves. I believe that if we can love ourselves unconditionally, the world will change for the better. Gandhi said, "Be the change you want to see in the world." It starts with me, and that is

Once we under-stand ourselves better, the next step is to accept the things we can't change and work positively on the things we can.

why it is my life's purpose to remember, honor, and treasure who I am through forgiveness, acceptance, and love.

When I was writing this book, I asked a few old-age homes and schools to contribute thoughts about love, and after going to collect these, I would give a short performance. I recently visited the André van der Walt Old Age Home in Bellville, South Africa, and had such an amazing time there. My husband and I prefer not to take our girls to work with us, but I took Kaeley, Jade, and Tayden that day, and I am so glad I did.

Caring starts with understanding ourselves.

When we arrived, the girls ran into the entertainment hall where all the old folks sat waiting for us, and Kaeley made herself at home on someone's lap while Jade and Tayden chatted excitedly to some friendly ladies in the front row. I called my girls onto the stage and we all sang "Tomorrow" (the theme song from *Annie*) for our loving audience, and to my surprise, my three-year-old girls sang as if they had done it a thousand times before. Kaeley even bowed with me to the warm applause we received after our performance. After that, we couldn't get Jade and Tayden off the stage; they kept dancing and running in circles behind me. I sang a few more songs holding Kaeley in my arms because she was feeling very emotional. Just like her mommy, she picked up on all the emotions in the hall and she felt a bit overwhelmed.

It starts with me, and that is why it is my life's purpose to remember, honor, and treasure who I am through forgiveness, acceptance, and love.

During my performance I talked to the audience about how most of us are so busy surviving that we are not really living. Afterward I hugged and greeted everyone as if they were my own grandparents. The love I felt was enormous. One lady grabbed me by the shoulders and excitedly confirmed that she was alive! Just before I left, one frail lady whispered into my ear, saying that she still had a lot to learn about unconditional love. I thought, *Me, too,* and there, in her loving embrace, I realized that we never stop learning. I have never felt so much love in one place, at one time. I know where to go if I need a love injection now.

Awareness is the birth of new beginnings, the beginning of a life worth living, the beginning of actually being alive. It's so easy to fall back into old habits and forget. That is why we should constantly engage in activities that remind us to remain in control of our fears and our lives.

> *Awareness is the birth of new beginnings, the beginning of a life worth living, the beginning of actually being alive.*

As a musician, I can't resist the urge to end this book with one last song. It came to me very late one night toward the end of 2006, and I remember crying as the words poured out of me. Realizing how I allowed fear to control my life made me feel very sad, but thankfully my eyes opened because of this song. I sing it about 100 times a year, but even that isn't enough to keep me aware, which is why I have dedicated my life to motivating and inspiring others. By doing this, I motivate and inspire myself so that I don't forget.

I am alive—finally!

FINALLY

I've been afraid for way too long,
Afraid to fail or to be wrong,
Afraid to be alive

But time has shown me who I am
And I have come to understand
That failing's not the end

And now the walls are slowly crumbling,
Nothing's left to hold me down
I can finally see that victory's inside of me,
My time has come and I know I must set myself free

'Cause I'm alive, finally,
There's no fear controlling me,
I'm alive finally, finally

'Cause I am here, it's all I have
And what I have I long to give,
So I give all of me
Embrace this love and take me,
Make me part of your life,
'Cause I'm already yours

And now the walls are slowly crumbling,
Nothing's left to hold me down
I can finally see that victory's inside of me,
My time has come and I know I must set myself free

'Cause I'm alive, finally,
There's no fear controlling me

Victory's inside of me,
There's nothing left to hold me down, I'm free

'Cause I'm alive, finally,
There's no fear controlling me,
I'm alive finally, finally

THANK YOU

First of all, I want to thank Struik Media for their interest and for getting me to write this book many years before I thought I would.

I would also like to thank the following institutions for participating and for their input on this book:

Schools: Curro Langebaan Private School; Laerskool Dirkie Uys, Mooreesburg; Liebenberg Primêr, Malmesbury; Laerskool Van Riebeeck-strand, Melkbosstrand; Laerskool Verkenner, Port Elizabeth; Laerskool Aristea, Kraaifontein

Old-age homes: Senior members from André van der Walt Home, Bell-ville; and Aristea Senior Home, Durbanville

To my dear friend Ronel Barkhuizen, thank you for all the time you've dedicated to this book. By now you can probably recite what I wrote by heart. Without your help and input, it would have taken me another year to finish. Your friendship is truly a blessing.

A special thanks to all the South African celebrities for their quotes on love. Mom and Dad, thank you for your love.

To my darling Andrew, thank you for all the nights you slept on the couch in the TV room so that I could write till the early hours of the morning. Your support and the fact that you always leave me the space to be who I am are the reasons why I fly. I love you always.

MY PRAYER

Dear God,
Thank you for guiding me to a knowing of who I am;
Thank you for helping me let go of my worldly expectations and to just be;
Thank you for freeing me from my ego so that I now give and love
unconditionally;
Thank you for filling me with your peace, joy, and love.
I love YOU.
Amen

ENDNOTES

CHAPTER 1: LOVING MYSELF AND ACCEPTING MY WORTH

1. Marianne Williamson, *A Return to Love: Reflections on the Principles of* A Course in Miracles, HarperCollins, 1992 (pp. 190–191).

CHAPTER 2: FOLLOWING MY DREAMS AND REACHING MY GOALS

1. Neale Donald Walsch, *Conversations with God,* G.P. Putnam's Sons, New York, 1996.

CHAPTER 3: BODY, MIND, AND SOUL

1. Louise L. Hay, *Heal Your Body,* Hay House, Inc., Carlsbad, Calif., 1988.
2. http://nianell.co.za/site/?page_id=489
   Maryke Bronkhorst: www.salveo.co.za
3. Nicolette Lodge, physical trainer and motivator:
   www.nicolettelodge.blogspot.com
4. www.quantumenergywellness.com/index-7.htm
   SCIO: www.scio.co.za
   www.sciohealth.com
5. www.metamorphosis-rstjohn.com
   www.metamorphictechnique.org

6. http://medical-dictionary.thefreedictionary.com/chiropracty

7. www.the-law-of-attraction-guide.com/louise-hay.html

8. http://nianell.co.za/site/?page_id=489
    Brain Gym®: www.braingym.org

9. From the Myers-Briggs Type Indicator test.

10. The Thomas-Kilmann Conflict Mode Instrument (TKI) is designed to assess an individual's behavior in conflict situations—that is, situations in which the concerns of two people appear to be incompatible. In such situations, we can describe a person's behavior along two basic dimensions: (1) Assertiveness, the extent to which the individual attempts to satisfy his or her own concerns; and (2) Cooperativeness, the extent to which the individual attempts to satisfy the other person's concerns.

11. Neale Donald Walsch, *Conversations with God,* G.P. Putnam's Sons, New York, 1996.

12. Louise L. Hay, *Heal Your Body,* Hay House, Inc., Carlsbad, Calif., 1988.

13. Hanna Kok, life coach and author: www.makealife.co.za

CHAPTER 4: RECONNECTING RELATIONSHIPS

1. Louise L. Hay, *Love Youself, Heal Your Life Workbook,* Hay House, Inc., Carlsbad, Calif., 1990.

2. Dr. Wayne Dyer, *Inspiration: Your Ultimate Calling,* Hay House, Inc., Carlsbad, Calif., 2006.

CHAPTER 5: THE MIRACLE OF THREE

1. Michael V. Hernandez, "Restating Implied, Prescriptive, and Statutory Easements," *Real Property, Probate and Trust Journal,* American Bar Association, Spring 2005, www.mayitpleasethecourt.com/journal.asp?blogID=898. (Accessed November 20, 2008.)

CHAPTER 7: MUSIC, MY TEACHER

1. John C. Maxwell, *Everyone Communicates, Few Connect: What the Most Effective People Do Differently,* Thomas Nelson, Nashville, Tennessee, 2010.

2. Anthony Robbins, *Awaken the Giant Within: How to Take Immediate Control of Your Mental, Emotional, Physical and Financial Destiny!*, Summit Books, New York, 1991.

3. Dr. Wayne Dyer, *Inspiration: Your Ultimate Calling*, Inspiration Cards, Hay House, Inc., Carlsbad, Calif., 2006.

4. http://www.musictherapy.org/faq/#38

RECOMMENDED READING

- *Tuesdays with Morrie*—Mitch Albom
- *Why Is God Laughing?*—Deepak Chopra
- *The Alchemist*—Paulo Coelho
- *The Power of Intention*—Dr. Wayne W. Dyer
- *A School Called Earth*—Luis Miguel Falcoa
- *Emotional Intelligence*—Daniel Goleman
- *Heal Your Body*—Louise L. Hay
- *You Can Heal Your Life*—Louise L. Hay
- *Happy Ever After*—Hanna Kok
- *Everyone Communicates, Few Connect*—John C. Maxwell
- *The Road Less Traveled*—M. Scott Peck
- *Healthy Kids*—Mary-Ann Shearer
- *The Natural Way*—Mary-Ann Shearer
- *A New Earth*—Eckhart Tolle
- *Conversations with God*—Neale Donald Walsch

ABOUT THE AUTHOR

Nianell is a gifted singer, a talented musician and songwriter, an author, and an inspirational keynote speaker. Often referred to as South Africa's version of Celine Dion, Nianell achieved international success with her song "Who Painted the Moon?" when Hayley Westenra did a cover version that sold over two million copies worldwide.

Other career highlights include a duet performance with the legendary tenor Andrea Bocelli during one of his visits to South Africa, along with a world-televised performance at the closing ceremony 2010 FIFA World Cup finals. In addition, Nianell has achieved gold status with four of her albums and platinum status with three, establishing her as one of South Africa's top-selling artists. Her music is a combination of folk, pop, country, and classical, ensuring that there is something for everybody in her diverse range of melodies.

Nianell exudes the very love and inspiration she sings about, and her passion and sincerity are contagious. Over and above reaching the top of the music game in South Africa, Nianell is also an astute businessperson and the mother of triplets.

Website: **www.nianell.com**
Facebook: **www.facebook.com/nianell**
Fan mail: nianell@nia.co.za

NIANELL
enterprises

To book Nianell, contact Andrew Thompson:
E-mail: nia@nia.co.za
Mobile: 00 27 (0)82 852 7067

NOTES

NOTES

NOTES

NOTES

NOTES

NOTES

NOTES

NOTES

HAY HOUSE TITLES
OF RELATED INTEREST

YOU CAN HEAL YOUR LIFE, *the movie,* starring Louise L. Hay & Friends
(available as a 1-DVD program and an expanded 2-DVD set)
Watch the trailer at: **www.LouiseHayMovie.com**

THE SHIFT, *the movie,* starring Dr. Wayne W. Dyer
(available as a 1-DVD program and an expanded 2-DVD set)
Watch the trailer at: **www.DyerMovie.com**

AMAZING GRACE, by Cecilia (CD)

GRACE, GUIDANCE, AND GIFTS: *Sacred Blessings to Light Your Way,*
by Sonia Choquette (book-with-CD)

UNITED BREAKS GUITARS: *The Power of One Voice in the Age of Social Media,*
by Dave Carroll (book)

WISHES FULFILLED: *Mastering the Art of Manifesting,*
by Dr. Wayne W. Dyer (book)

YOU CAN CREATE AN EXCEPTIONAL LIFE,
by Louise Hay and Cheryl Richardson (book)

All of the above are available at your local bookstore,
or may be ordered by contacting Hay House (see next page).

We hope you enjoyed this Hay House book. If you'd like to receive our online catalog featuring additional information on Hay House books and products, or if you'd like to find out more about the Hay Foundation, please contact:

Hay House, Inc., P.O. Box 5100, Carlsbad, CA 92018-5100
(760) 431-7695 or (800) 654-5126
(760) 431-6948 (fax) or (800) 650-5115 (fax)
www.hayhouse.com® • **www.hayfoundation.org**

Published and distributed in Australia by: Hay House Australia Pty. Ltd.,
18/36 Ralph St., Alexandria NSW 2015 • *Phone:* 612-9669-4299
Fax: 612-9669-4144 • www.hayhouse.com.au

Published and distributed in the United Kingdom by: Hay House UK, Ltd.,
292B Kensal Rd., London W10 5BE • *Phone:* 44-20-8962-1230
Fax: 44-20-8962-1239 • www.hayhouse.co.uk

Published in India by: Hay House Publishers India, Muskaan Complex, Plot
No. 3, B-2, Vasant Kunj, New Delhi 110 070 • *Phone:* 91-11-4176-1620
Fax: 91-11-4176-1630 • www.hayhouse.co.in

Distributed in Canada by: Raincoast, 9050 Shaughnessy St., Vancouver, B.C.
V6P 6E5 • *Phone:* (604) 323-7100 • *Fax:* (604) 323-2600 • www.raincoast.com

Take Your Soul on a Vacation
Visit **www.HealYourLife.com®** to regroup, recharge, and reconnect with
your own magnificence. Featuring blogs, mind-body-spirit news, and
life-changing wisdom from Louise Hay and friends.

Visit **www.HealYourLife.com** today!

Free Mind~Body~Spirit e~Newsletters

From Hay House, the Ultimate Resource for Inspiration

Be the first to know about Hay House's dollar deals, free downloads, special offers, affirmation cards, giveaways, contests, and more!

 Get exclusive excerpts from our latest releases and videos from *Hay House Present Moments*.

 Enjoy uplifting personal stories, how-to articles, and healing advice, along with videos and empowering quotes, within *Heal Your Life*.

 Have an inspirational story to tell and a passion for writing? Sharpen your writing skills with insider tips from *Your Writing Life*.

Receive uplifting affirmations, empowering thoughts, and healing wisdom from *Louise Hay*.

Discover ways to overcome all obstacles with the inspiring words of *Dr. Wayne Dyer* to get your wishes fulfilled.

Get angelic, heavenly assistance for your everyday life from angel expert and lifelong clairvoyant *Doreen Virtue*.

Uncover the timeless secrets of life from *Gregg Braden* and discover the collective wisdom of our past.

**Get inspired, educate yourself, and share the wisdom!
Visit www.hayhouse.com to sign up today!**